Controlled Capitalism

(Capitalism or Socialism in 2004?)

By

Warren E. Peterson

ISBN: 1-4140-2258-1 (e-book)
ISBN: 1-4140-2257-3 (Paperback)
ISBN: 1-4140-2256-5 (Dust Jacket)

Library of Congress Control Number: 2003097999

This book is printed on acid free paper.

Printed in the United States of America
Bloomington, IN

1stBooks—rev. 01/19/04

Table of Contents

Introduction

Capitalism is an economic system which materially rewards the individual based upon their talents and aspiration in life. If not controlled by the people through the government, however, capitalism can be an economic system in which the financially strong dominate the financially weak, thus resulting in the exploitation of the weak. Economic systems are created for people; people are not created for economic systems. An economic system will serve the people or the people will change it, either by ballot or bullet. The recent fall of communism in the Soviet Union and the eastern European countries are examples of this viewpoint. The effort to have capitalism in Russia is still on trial.

Some of the people and events which occurred from the late 1880s to today are presented here to provide a history of capitalism in America. They describe some of the positive aspects of capitalism and, also, the negative features of capitalism and how the American people responded to those events to make a positive change within the capitalistic economic system in America.

The result of that response is the highest standard of living for any country and it's people in the history of mankind. The intent of these writings is to challenge the leaders and people in America to look seriously at the economic system we have in place. Our individual political freedom, coupled with our controlling capitalism through legislation to prevent exploitation of the people, must be preserved.

My paternal grandparents emigrated from Sweden in the early 1880s and settled in St. Paul, Minnesota. They placed their trust in God and the country they had chosen to reap the rewards of their labor. With those rewards, they raised a family of four daughters and one son (my father). The awareness of the reward which comes from hard work and the fulfillment of individual responsibility were taught to their children. These same values were passed by my father to his children. We were taught that only our individual abilities and desires were the limiting factors as to what standard of living each of us could achieve.

I realized later in life that some of the citizens of America were deprived of the same opportunity but that issue was addressed in the 1960s and subsequent years. Today the government assures all Americans of the opportunity to use their abilities and desires to achieve a higher standard of living. It all depends upon each individual's effort. That opportunity was accomplished without destroying capitalism in America.

Ideals concerning social and moral responsibilities were taught to both my parents by their fathers and mothers. With those same values presented to me by my parents, I have had an interest in the way we should treat other people who are occupying this world with us. As a result of that interest, I decided to research our history to determine why the people in the United States have been blessed with such an abundance of material wealth while the people in a large number of countries throughout the remainder of the world have failed to do so.

Many of the questions which were in my head were answered while reading five books. The first book was A People's History of the United States (1492-present). It was written by Howard Zinn and published by HarperPerennial. Much of the material necessary to confirm the views and conclusions you will find in these writings was found in his book. Many people consider Howard Zinn to be of the liberal political persuasion. At times, during the reading of his book, this bias was quite apparent to me but I looked past it when I saw how well documented his book was. His liberal bias, coupled with my moderate to conservative views, prompted me to weigh carefully some of the conclusions I reached.

A second book which proved of value during the research was Who Built America? (Volume Two) which was an American Social History Project published by Pantheon Books. The book is a very well documented and factual presentation by several writers of events which occurred during the period that is the focus of these writings. It was the most important of all the books I read in helping me confirm my thoughts for my writings. The authors wrote about the events and people which were a very important part of our development into the most powerful free capitalist country in the world. My writings refer to the single topic of controlled capitalism and how the people, entrepreneurs, and government have worked to create this great country. What is so unique about their effort is how the many different views expressed by all involved have, so far, enabled most Americans to enjoy a comfortable standard of living while continuing to allow capitalism to flourish. Don't Know Much About History is another book from which I gathered information. It was written by Kenneth C. Davis and published by Avon Books which is a division of The Hearst Corporation.

A fourth book which was very helpful in gaining insight into the topic chosen for these writings was A History of the American People. It was written by Paul Johnson and originally published in Great Britain in 1997 by Weidenfeld & Nicolson. The First HarperPerennial edition which I used was published in 1999. In the dedication which is written by Johnson, it is stated "This book is dedicated to the people of America—strong, outspoken, intense in their convictions, sometimes wrong-headed but always generous and brave, with a passion for justice no nation has ever matched". It was his opinion of the American people which influenced me to read the book. I felt he knew us very well.

The fifth book used as a reference was the Almanac of American History which was published by Barnes & Noble, Inc. by arrangement with Putnam Grosset Group. Arthur M. Schlesinger, Jr. was the General Editor and it was copyright by Brompton Books Corporation in 1993. The book records the events in America's history by day, month and year which enabled me to obtain more thorough information from the previously mentioned books by knowing the time periods in which to concentrate my research.

Obviously, it was necessary for me to research the early days of capitalism in America to present how it developed as the economic system in the United States. Each book provided me with the people and events necessary to coordinate the views expressed in these writings. Some of the people and events were more fully covered in certain of the books than the others. That is why you will find the references in the Source Notes appear to be heavily referenced towards a particular book during a certain presentation of a person or event. I confess that without the knowledge from the above five books, and a few Internet sites, this book would have been impossible for me to write. Though I am an avid history reader, it was impossible for me to pull all of the information I have read over the years out of my head. However, once I reached the period of time in which I was involved in the business world as a Department Manager, much of the views expressed are from personal experience. From the time period of the mid to late 1950s, I relied less and less upon information from the above mentioned books and have expressed views based upon the knowledge I acquired while observing events as they unfolded during my adult life.

To the publishers and writers of the above mentioned books, I extend my greatest appreciation. It is not my intention to plagiarize any of their writings. If at times, it appears a reference was not placed in the Source Notes, it is simply an oversight and I apologize. If you, the reader, are interested in the history of America, it is my recommendation that you read the books to which I referred above. You will receive an excellent education about all of our history and not just one concerning a specific item such as capitalism. If we do not know the history of our country, we will undo the good things and repeat the bad things. In my opinion, you will not find the books to be mundane reading.

With the individual responsibility beliefs instilled into me by my father, I feel confident in expressing my view about how to help adult people who are in need, but also how to not make them slaves of the government when such care is provided. To give government money to an individual without requiring that person to develop work skills through technical schools or obtaining further education while receiving such funds, is one of the most unkind acts a government can bestow upon anyone. Without increasing their ability to become self-sufficient, the adult individual will always be indentured to the government, thus losing out on the opportunity to reach the material standard of living which is available to all people in the United States of America through our system of capitalism. That is why I have a negative bias towards President Lyndon B. Johnson's Great Society Program. Many of the programs required nothing in return for the money provided to individuals. For the overall benefit of our social structure, a "second chance opportunity" should be afforded to an adult individual who was not mature enough to understand the importance of an education when they were an adolescent. As a result, they lack the skills to obtain gainful employment. Once they have received further education, the individual should then be responsible for their own future.

I am an example of a "second chance" from society. After serving four years in the US Navy during the Korean War, I had matured enough to realize it would be beneficial for me to receive more education. In September 1955, I enrolled at the University of Cincinnati. With the help of the G.I. Bill money which was available to me, I attended the Evening College for five years while working during the day. As I studied to receive an Associate Degree in Factory Management, I was able to see how the theories which I was being taught were put into action within the business world. The company for which I worked while attending college, had placed me in the position of Production Control Manager. Through that position, and later the Purchasing Manager position, I attained knowledge and experience about labor/management relations and the need for a company to be profitable so it would be capable of providing jobs for society. (As an aside, society benefitted greatly by their investment in me through the G.I. Bill. The taxes I paid over the years because of my positions were many ten's of thousands of dollars greater than the amount of government money I had received.)

During those years of working within the capitalistic system, I was able to observe how different capitalists responded to capitalism in different ways. My observation led me to conclude that most capitalists were law abiding citizens. Because a few ran their companies in an unethical manner, special interest groups pressured the government to police the activities of all capitalists. Legislature and congressional bodies enacted laws which would have been unnecessary had those few capitalists been better corporate citizens.

The profit motive of capitalism is also a subject of which I have considerable understanding. Without profits, whether it be capitalism, socialism, or communism, any economic system will be unable to provide jobs for their citizenry over a lasting period. The fall of Communism in the Soviet Union is an example of this viewpoint. No company is entitled to a profit, though. They must earn it. It is my opinion, based upon several decades of observation, government bureaucracy is incapable of providing an efficient profit-oriented economic system. When the political environment is also the production environment, there are no checks and balances available to prevent costly and harmful waste. Therefore, in such a scenario, the production efforts by a company will continue to operate for political reasons even though the company will not contribute anything to society. Socialism and communism are examples of such economic systems.

In capitalism, a company which does not have good management skills within the management personnel will fail and go out of business. This may sound very "cold" but that is a necessary event which must occur to assure an efficient work environment which will benefit all of society. To support that viewpoint, I refer to the "Peter Principle" where people advance to their level of incompetency at which point they fail.

Serving for three years as the Treasurer and Secretary of a political party's County Executive Committee, enabled me to meet political leaders of both national parties at all levels of our government. The knowledge gained by these relationships helped me to understand how the political forces are at work within the United States and how representative government works.

Capitalism has succeeded in America, up to this point, as a result of the government allowing individuals to be the entrepreneurs who provide the jobs through which other Americans are able to become part of the greatest standard of living in the history of the world. Some of the unethical characteristics of the early years of capitalism, however, have resurfaced in America during recent years. People who believe in capitalism must speak out today to preserve it as an economic system which is best for America and the world. Severe punishment should be given to those business and labor leaders who have betrayed the trust which was bestowed upon them by the people of America. We must let the rest of the world understand that capitalism is an economic system under which people can achieve a comfortable life style but it must be controlled within a political system of freedom.

In these writings, it is my objective to draw attention to the struggles of the American workers who were seeking to obtain a greater share of the wealth which was being created by their productivity. Today we are living in a society where we are reaping the rewards of those who fought to control capitalism in America but did not destroy it. We should strive to continue this legacy which was given to us by our ancestors.

Chapter 1

American Capitalists in Late 1800s

The need for the necessary capital to produce goods for consumption by a growing middle class began to develop in the early 1800s. The invention of the machinery required to produce these goods for the growing consumer market brought the need for capital. Entrepreneurs needed capital to manufacture the machinery and the producers of the goods to be sold likewise required capital to purchase the machinery. Individuals with financial resources became known as capitalists as they began providing the capital sought by those who developed the ideas of how to produce and distribute those goods. As the amount of capital needed to meet the demand increased, the desire to be more protective of the money being loaned by the bankers grew greater. The solution the bankers introduced to better protect their money was to reduce competition, organize the businesses and move toward a monopoly of the business community.[1]

Those same individuals also sought to minimize their risks by making certain the government's role would be to help the business interests in America. This view was similar to that which Alexander Hamilton and the First Congress had advocated.[2] Those individuals with monetary wealth began to control the political activity in America for their personal gains. Control, through bribery, of influential leaders in congressional and legislative bodies throughout the United States became their objective. For many years, those influential legislators worked to protect the interest of the bankers and industrialists. Through those legislators, laws which were proposed by fellow legislators who wished to advanced the interests of the workers were prevented from becoming law. Instead, laws were passed which allowed for further exploitation of the workers. The wealth of the bankers and industrialists increased while the workers were negatively affected by such laws. While the wealthy bankers and industrialists enjoyed the life of luxury, the workers remained in very low economic surroundings due to the restrictions on labor activities and low pay.

Among those industrialists and bankers were Cornelius Vanderbilt (1794-1877), Jay Gould (1836—92), Andrew Carnegie (1835-1919), J.P. Morgan (1837-1913) and John D. Rockefeller (1839-1937) who, alleged by historians, established business empires through bribes of political and governmental positions. In his book, A History of the American People, Paul Johnson writes about these five giants who became known as the Robber Barons.[3] Not all industrialists and bankers in America used corrupt methods but the conduct of the Robber Barons pointed out the need to control capitalism by controlling the activities of the capitalists.

It is my view Johnson describes their background and actions in such a manner that an individual can reach their own conclusion as to whether the allegations leveled against them are true or false. They are included in these writings as examples of why capitalism as an economic system must be allowed to succeed but it should be controlled to prevent the exploitation of society as a whole. After all, society is both the producer of goods and the consumer of those goods.

Johnson begins his presentation of these five individuals by stating that Cornelius Vanderbilt was the first of the big-time tycoons but he started as a boatman. When he was seventeen, his mother loaned him $100 to buy a two-masted barge known as a leriauger and he used it as a ferry. Following that he became involved in water-transport. At age 21, he had been successful in acquiring $10,000 in capital which he used to break the monopoly of the Fulton-Livingstone combine on the Hudson by operating the unlicenced Bellano. American businessmen would break the law if they considered the law as monopolistic. They did not show respect toward monopolies in the same manner the English did for the monopoly charters awarded by parliamentary statue.[4]

The Supreme Court declared the Hudson Water a monopoly, thus the law which made it possible was declared unconstitutional. Vanderbilt came to see laws as something that favored any group of businessmen who would bribe state legislatures or hire expensive lawyers in an effort to win court decisions for them. With that belief, he began to bribe judges, even bribe whole state legislatures, and once obtained aid from the federal government when he had the use of entire regiments of marines while operating in Latin America.

When he began to develop plans for a fast route to California by sea, he not only had the use of marine regiments provided by the United States government but he also bought up the government of Nicaragua. This was necessary to obtain the use of Nicaragua's land for the overland part of the journey. The experience he gained as a result of the railroad project on the land part of his California fast route, enabled him to become a knowledgeable investor in the railroad system in the United States. He was successful in purchasing the New York Central Railroad.[5] A Robber Baron? You decide.

On October 8, 1867, Jay Gould met two individuals named Daniel Drew and Jim Fisk. Unlike the other two, Gould had "class" but he likewise lacked integrity. Gould had come up through the tanning and leather industry. After deciding on a career in Wall Street, he became an expert in railroad stock which would benefit him later. Drew had been a cattle-driver and would drive herds of 1,000 head to the selling point. There he would salt them and fill them up with water before selling. This became known as "watered stock" which was a phrase he took with him when he too went to Wall Street. Fisk began in the money game by buying up cotton in occupied areas of the South, then selling it in the North. He then decided to sell almost worthless Confederate bonds in England. He was said to be "able to spot a sucker at a hundred yards" and coined the phrase "never give a sucker an even break".[6]

It was during Vanderbilt's quest for more railroad ownership that he encountered the business "talents" of Jay Gould and his friends. When Gould teamed up with Drew and Fisk, they decided on a stock raid to take over the Erie Railroad. Vanderbilt had been attempting to acquire the railroad but was prevented to do so by the tactics which the three partners used. They would send the Erie stock price up and down by selling and buying at different levels. When the price of the stock would hit a low point, they would move in and buy a large number of shares.

Vanderbilt attempted to obstruct their activities by having Judge George C. Barnard, a member of the Tweed Ring run by Boss Tweed of Tammany Hall, give him an injunction which would prevent them from running the stock prices up and down. At the time, Barnard was in Vanderbilt's pay. Gould countered this attempt by Vanderbilt by throwing 100,000 shares into the market. The price exploded like a mine and in Drew's phrase, "Erie went down like a dead heifer."[7]

Gould and Drew were later forced out of ownership of the Erie Railroad after it was discovered they had bribed the New York legislature to legalize their issue of $8 million in "watered stock" on the Erie Railroad.[8] There is no question but that Gould, Drew and Fisk milked the Erie Railroad which had been a profitable railroad. In 1877, Erie was forced to file for bankruptcy and was restored to solvency only after a series of reorganizations. It was not until 1942 that the railroad was able to pay any dividends.[9] This is an example how uncontrolled capitalism harmed a large number of persons, i.e. workers, lenders and shareholders. The Security Exchange Commission had not yet been created by the government.

During the term of President U.S. Grant, Gould, Drew and Fisk were involved in the gold scandal which was contrived by Gould. The scheme was to "corner" the gold market. In May 1869, Gould met Abel Rathbone Corbin, who was married to Grant's sister. Gould knew that Corbin was concerned about the plight of the farmers. With that knowledge, he pointed out to Corbin how well the farmers had prospered during the Civil War inflation. Gold, at that time, would buy $2.50 of paper money. To raise the gold price and lower the value of the dollar, Western grain crops would move rapidly and be sold in Europe. The scheme would be good for the West and at the same time it would be good for the individuals who promoted it. He offered Corbin $1.3 million of gold at 133 on credit.[10]

Gould began buying gold in June on his and his friends' accounts and continued through August. Gold was also bought for General Daniel Butterfield who was the Assistant Secretary of the U.S. Treasury. A check for $25,000 on account was given to Corbin for "profits to come". In return for the money, Corbin told Gould on September 2 that he had personally witnessed President Grant signing a specific order to U.S. Treasury Secretary George Sewell Boutwell which prohibited him from selling gold without direct orders from the President.[11]

Funds that Gould had acquired from the Tenth National Bank, which was controlled by Tammany Hall, were used to purchase $40 million of gold by September 22. This was twice the amount which was usually in circulation. Horace Greeley's New York Tribune began to demand that the U.S. Treasury sell gold as the dollar was inflating to unsatisfactory levels. Grant, upon receiving news of what was happening to the price of gold, immediately issued a verbal order to the Treasury to begin selling gold. They were to continue the selling until the "corner" was broken.

On September 24, 1869, gold opened at 142 and went up to 162. Gould and his friends began selling into the highly volatile gold market. It is not known whether they made or lost money with their sales that day but by the end of the day, a stock-market panic had begun which turned into a Depression that lasted for several years. An interesting story came out of this gold market event. When the bell of Wall Street's Trinity Church started to strike noon on that day, the price of gold was 160. By the time the bells fell silent, the price was 138. President Grant became suspicious of his brother-in-law, Corbin, and immediately broke off relations with him.[12]

The acts of Gould and his friends demonstrated the need for the government, as a voice of the people, to prevent unscrupulous people from orchestrating such activities. In this particular case, nothing was done to prevent it from occurring in the future. Naming Gould as one of the Robber Barons is merited based upon his many unscrupulous business activities.

The third individual who is alleged to have been one of the Robber Barons is Andrew Carnegie. He was born in Dunfermline, Scotland in 1835 and emigrated with his father's family to the United States in 1848 at age thirteen. The Carnegie family settled in a Scottish neighborhood in Pittsburgh which was a small industrial outpost in western Pennsylvania. To help the family, he worked twelve hours a day as a bobbin-boy for $1.50 a week. Always looking for better opportunities, he took a job as telegraph messenger with Western Union where he earned $2.50 a week.[13]

Western Union was a company of opportunity which enabled Carnegie to become the personal telegrapher and assistant to Thomas Scott. Scott was the superintendent of the Pennsylvania Railroad's

Western Division. In 1859, Scott was promoted to Pennsylvania Railroad as a vice-president. Carnegie, though he was only twenty-four, was given Scott's job of superintendent. This was when Carnegie discovered the delights of capitalism. Having invested his earnings for a period of time, he had an annual income of $47,860.67 of which only $2,500 was his salary. The rest was profits from the investments he had made. Deciding that working for others was not the best way to increase his income, he looked around for a position which would provide him with a higher income.[14] With the knowledge he had gained about railroad operations, he decided to go to Wall Street where he sold railroad bonds for huge commissions. He soon became a millionaire through those commissions.[15]

With the rich iron ore fields found around Lake Superior, coupled with the large amount of Pennsylvania anthracite coal deposits and cheap water-transport and power of the region, it was assured that the region would become the center of America's heavy industry. His knowledge of the region provided him with the foresight of what to do with his new fortune. In 1872, Carnegie went to London where he saw the new Bessemer method of producing steel. He returned to America and built a million-dollar steel plant in Pittsburgh.[16]

Carnegie quickly discovered that the Bessemer and the open hearth Siemans-Martin methods of making steel, while good, were imperfectly understood. That was when he put his laboratory technicians to work and began associating chemistry with steel-production. Between 1880 and 1900, U.S. steel production rose from 1.25 million tons to over 10 million tons annually. Carnegie's furnaces produced nearly one-third of the nation's output. His iron and steel products set the standards for quality and price. The price leadership was possible through the control of unit costs. He felt there should be an accounting of the costs at each step of production. This would identify those areas of cost which could be reduced through better management. Methods which would improve productivity were established, thus enabling him to lower prices and still maintain the profitability of his company.[17]

Tremendous personal wealth came under his leadership. The wealth brought a personal conflict within Carnegie which was a result of the two views taught him during his childhood. His mother had

6

taught him thrift. The lessons of life he learned by being poor during his childhood made him determined to take care of his family and assure them of a better life now that he had wealth. This compelled him to continue increasing his wealth. His father had lost his job as a hand-loom weaver to make way for power looms. It was then he had taught a young Andrew the importance of new technology. As a political activist, he also instilled in his son the value of political and economic equality. The most prominent black mark on Carnegie's career was the Homestead Strike which will be discussed later.

Because Carnegie's wealth and the ghosts of his father's radical past troubled him, he wrote himself a letter early in his career. In that letter, he promised that he would stop working in two more years after which he would pursue a life of good works. He stated, "To continue much longer overwhelmed by business cares...must degrade me beyond hope of permanent recovery". Yet Carnegie's business cares continued to demand his attention. For three decades he dominated the steel industry, and although he allowed himself time for vacations in Scotland and also for his troubled courtship of Louise Whitfield, his thoughts rarely strayed from his mills.[18]

The conflict within himself surfaced when he encountered the Amalgamated Association of Iron and Steel Workers union in his mills. He publicly supported unions because of the inner desire for political and economic equality. However, he wanted a labor force within his own enterprise which would work for whatever wages and working conditions he offered without his employees questioning them. The workers in the Homestead Works earned wages which were one-third higher than other steel mills. He knew the only way to achieve his goal of a complacent and non-challenging work force was to break the Amalgamated Association of Iron and Steel Workers union. The effort to break the union will be presented later when the conflicts between workers and entrepreneurs will be discussed.

During a dinner in 1901 which both Carnegie and J.P. Morgan were attending, Morgan said he was interested in Carnegie's company. When asked how much he wanted for the company, Carnegie wrote $492,000,000 on a note. Perhaps Carnegie saw an opportunity to finally fulfill the promise he had made to himself years before. Morgan agreed to the price and combined Carnegie's corporations with others he controlled.

To finance the purchase, Morgan sold $1.3 billion worth of stocks and bonds from which he took a commission of $150 million for arranging the consolidation. The next step taken to enhance the consolidation was to have Congress pass tariffs that kept out foreign steel which prevented competition. This enabled him to maintain a price of $28 a ton. His workforce of 200,000 were also forced to endure working twelve hours a day at a wage level which made it difficult for the families of the workers to cope.[19]

After selling his company, Carnegie began to use his energies through philanthropy. Perhaps he thought this would make amends to society for the manner in which he had accumulated his fortune. As a result of this philanthropy, he is most remembered for his gifts of music halls, educational grants, and approximately 3,000 public libraries. His philanthropy makes it difficult for me to place him among the Robber Barons.

He may have acquired his wealth through self-centered views involving his workers and business practices, but he returned the wealth to society in a manner which benefits the people of America even to this day. The money to accomplish these lasting gifts came from a capitalist and not from the government which would have had to use money acquired from the public in the form of taxes for such accomplishments. The bureaucracy of government would have had to debate for many, many years to decide how to best use the money taxed from the public. I applaud him for his willingness to provide the capital for the many lasting gifts he bestowed upon America. The determination of whether he should have been included on the list of Robber Barons is left to each of the readers.

The above mentioned J.P. Morgan was another giant who was alleged to be a Robber Baron. He was a banker whose family already had a large fortune. His career began as a lawyer and banker in his father's international banking firm of J.S. Morgan and Company. It was during the Black Friday Panic of 1869 and subsequent Depression that Morgan took advantage of the situation and began to purchase the many railroads in America which were close to bankruptcy. With the stock of the railroads at very low prices, it was possible for him to acquire almost fifty percent of the railroads. He persuaded several of his friends to purchase the stocks of the remaining railroad companies. When they had completed the purchases, it enabled them to fix freight rates at scandalously high levels.

There was little the shippers could do about the high prices. An attempt to prevent these high shipping rates by governmental legislation was ruled against by the Supreme Court. It ruled that property cannot be taken away without due process of law. Since profits were considered property, the legislation was declared unconstitutional. With the high rates allowed to remain, the shippers had to pay the freight rates to ship their products to the marketplace in a timely fashion. Further study would have to be done by the government to determine how to prevent such monopolies in the future.

Many stories which were written about J.P. Morgan were done so by journalists who were looking for negative aspects of his life. Some of them were proven to be fabrications or were written in such a fashion as to strive to discredit him. It was reported that he speculated against the federal currency - so did everyone who could. He reportedly paid $300 for a substitute to serve in the federal draft. So, also, did everyone with the cash - the Civil War was indeed a rich man's war and a poor man's fight.[19]

Morgan was the only member of the New York financial community who was trusted by everyone else. With that trust came power and responsibility. He developed much of the financial structures in America because of this trust. The development of these financial structures are an example of his contribution to America's prominence without ever having been elected to a political office. The concentration of wealth was a concept he believed in but declared it should be used for the overall development of a strong economy in America which would benefit all Americans.[20]

There are three basic services which must be provided by any government. First, it must provide an external defense, second it must uphold law and order within the country, and third the currency which is provided must be looked upon by the rest of the world as an honest currency. The two oceans on each side provided defense which was helpful since there was not a strong military presence as part of the defense program. There was no national police program and in a great portion of the country there was no policing established.

To make matters worse, there was no central bank and those involved in the currency were divided about what did constitute the currency of the United States. Because of this latter fact, it was necessary to have unofficial arbiters who did establish and maintain standards pertaining to currency. Fortunately someone like J.P. Morgan was available to help in this task.[21] To those three, I would add one more responsibility of a government which would promote stability within its population. To assure everyone the opportunity to acquire the necessary knowledge to become a productive citizen, the government should provide a basic education. This can be accomplished by providing public education for grades 1 through 12 as has been done in America.

There were two occasions when the influence of Morgan was used to preserve the financial stability of America. In 1893, President Grover Cleveland asked him to come up with a plan which would solve the problem of the country's diminishing gold stock. Morgan's plan consisted of forming a syndicate which would market U.S. securities in Europe in return for gold. The plan proved to be successful when the outflow of gold from the United States was curbed.[22]

It was during the 1907 Panic that Morgan confronted the near collapse of the financial center of the United States. He met with his partners first to discuss what was occurring. Next he met with financial and business leaders in his mansion to determine the seriousness of the problem. After recognizing how serious the crisis was, he formed a team of young men who were immediately put to work. They were to review the accounts overnight and identify which of the big financial houses were too weak to save and must be allowed to collapse as well as those houses which could be rescued.

Once that was completed, he began raising liquidity by contacting bankers and urging them to provide the money which would be loaned without delay at ten percent. He also was able to obtain a commitment from the U.S. Treasury to provide funds to assist in the prevention of the collapse of America's financial center. The panic on the Stock Exchange began to subside when they knew there was money available to be loaned to them, even though it was at a high rate of interest. One or two of the big financial houses were allowed to fall but the overwhelming majority survived. The fundamentals of this rescue became the basis for the forming of the U.S. Federal Reserve Bank in 1914.[23]

An adverse aspect of J.P. Morgan's business activities, in my opinion, was the manner in which he and his friends purchased almost all of the railroads and then charged the exorbitant shipping fees. The ultimate payees of those rates were the consumers who were already subject to a much lower standard of living than he and his friends. Even though the Supreme Court ruled in his favor to nullify the legislative attempt to overturn the rates, he should have stepped back, reexamined his decision and then rescinded some of the increase he had put in place. That he was instrumental in the overall success in rescuing the financial structures which saved America's financial world from collapsing makes it difficult for me to place him among the Robber Barons. You, the reader, decide for yourself, though.

John D. Rockefeller, who was also alleged to be one of the Robber Barons, made his fortune in the oil industry. Very early in his life he discovered it was better to make your money work for you instead of you working for money. He learned this when he loaned a farmer $50 at an interest rate of seven percent. After studying bookkeeping, he was prepared to make his move into greater wealth. The first opportunity to make a major jump in his income came in 1862. A group of investors sent him to Oil Creek in Ohio to investigate the future of the newly discovered black liquid. The report he submitted to the investors falsely stated there was no future. He then proceeded to invest his money in one of the very first oil refineries.[24]

In 1867, Rockefeller united five refineries into one company which was called Rockefeller, Andrew and Flagler. Three years later, in 1870, the three of them reorganized the company and gave it the name Standard Oil of Ohio. This was done to obtain more capital which would be used to create another company. It is alleged that in 1871, with $1,000,000 capital they had raised, the South Improvement Company was organized as a transportation company with unrestricted statutory powers. This was chartered by the Pennsylvania legislature which Rockefeller had pressured into doing so. Rockefeller had no qualms about bribing legislatures to gain advantages which would benefit his business empire.[25]

It backfired though, as the new company quickly gained a reputation of conducting its business in an unfair manner. He used secret tactics by offering to transport large amounts of refined oil on the Erie, the New York Central, and the Pennsylvania railroads in return for special low rates and rebates. This created hardships for other refineries who were not afforded the same low rates by the railroads. When the rival oil companies became weak, Rockefeller would buy them out by using Standard Oil of Ohio stock. However, the practice of secret deals with the railroads by South Improvement Company caused such a protest by the public that Congress dissolved the company within three months of being chartered. That did not prevent Standard Oil of Ohio from having an almost complete monopoly of the refining capacity in America. This occurred at a time when the use of oil by the growing industrial community was expanding.[24]

In his book Don't Know Much About History, Kenneth C. Davis writes that twenty years later Standard had been transformed into a "holding company" with diversified interests. It was an attorney by the name of Samuel C.T. Dodd who was employed by Rockefeller that came up with the idea of "Trusts" in the business world. Standard Oil was an Ohio corporation. Ohio state law prohibited Standard Oil from owning plants in other states or holding stock in out-of-state corporations. Dodd developed "Trusts" by setting up a nine-man board of trustees. Instead of a corporation which issued stock, Standard Oil became a Trust which issued "Trust certificates". Through this method, Rockefeller acquired the entire oil refinery industry without breaking corporate anti-monopoly laws. The idea spread throughout the business world. By the early 1890s, more than 5,000 separate companies had been organized into 300 Trusts.[26]

Some may argue that a monopoly such as Standard Oil was good for society as a whole. Rockefeller had reduced the price of kerosene almost seventy percent. At that time almost every household in America used kerosene, thus making the lower prices beneficial to society. However, the wages of the workers were held down by the many monopolistic "Trusts" which had been formed in America. This prevented any advancement in the standard of living for lower class citizens while the upper middle class's sky-rocketed. Only the elite were capable of truly advancing their standard of living because of the monopolies which had been created through the "Trusts".[27]

The readers can reach their own conclusion as to whether John D. Rockefeller was correctly characterized as one of the Robber Barons by his actions or was he an astute businessman. It is worth considering whether an individual has gained his wealth by leaving the mass of society in the wake of his success or has he pulled the same society to success with him. Rockefeller was intent on becoming the richest man in the United States and possibly in the world. He accomplished this goal by being ruthless in his business practices of forcing other businessmen to sell their business to him at a reduced price or face total destruction. The other businessmen were deprived of the opportunity for individual success because of his power.

In their business practices, those individuals who were called Robber Barons were examples of the negative side of capitalists. Though they were responsible for a tremendous increase in the industrialization of America, they had done so through the exploitation of the workers who performed the tasks of production. Many of the workers in America were satisfied with the opportunity to have employment where they could provide a living, though a meager one, for their families but were not satisfied with the disparity between the growing number of wealthy individuals and the increasing number of people who were impoverished. A growing sentiment among the workers was that something had to be done to obtain a greater share of the wealth which was being produced in America.

The five individuals who were given the title of Robber Baron were aggressive individuals. Through that personality trait, they were able to accumulate a tremendous amount of wealth. Some did so through corruption of the political and judicial systems of America. However, to state that fact does not describe them as evil persons. Public environment at the time was one which encouraged such activity. The individuals were unable to understand that their living in extravagant styles while their employees were forced to live in inadequate conditions was basically an immoral activity towards others. Had they been more caring for their employees, capitalism would not have become a system which was looked upon with repugnance.

America had become known as the opportunity to go from "rags to riches" during this period. This myth had been created by the Horatio Alger stories of successful entrepreneurs. A study of the origins of 303 textile, railroad, and steel executives of the 1870s disproved this myth. It showed that 90 percent came from middle or upper class families.[28] Two examples of individuals who did not come from middle or upper class families were Thomas Edison and Henry Ford.

Howard Zinn pointed out in his book, A People's History of the United States 1492 to present, that "most of the fortune building was done legally, with the collaboration of the government and the courts. Sometimes the collaboration had to be paid for. Thomas Edison promised New Jersey politicians $1,000 each in return for favorable legislation."[29] To my knowledge, Henry Ford did not resort to such a practice. Despite the accusation against Edison, the entrepreneurial talents of these two individuals led to the formation of companies which have survived into the 21st century. Their creative ideas had a major impact upon the standard of living in America.

Thomas A. Edison (1847-1931) was born in Milan, Ohio. He had only three months of education in a school but his schoolteacher mother taught him at home until he was 12. He began selling newspapers on a railroad route to obtain money which he spent on his experiments. When he was 21, he worked in a brokerage house in New York. It was there where Edison, who had earlier mastered the workings of telegraphy, made significant changes to the stock tickers which improved the operation of the tickers. He sold the rights of the improvement for $40,000 and began a career as a free-lance inventor.[30] The first invention he had received a patent for was in 1869 and his ingenuity enabled him to have 1,328 patents registered by 1910.[31]

Edison had work habits which some may consider extreme. He worked tirelessly day and night on his projects at his laboratory where he ate and slept and required the same of his employees. There was little time for his nor his employees families. To work for him was to accept his extreme work habits or leave. In my opinion, Edison did a great injustice to the families of his employees by his extreme lifestyle. In today's political/labor climate, it would have been difficult for him to work his staff in the manner he did. Since the decision to continue working under such demands was an individual choice, each of his employees had to make such a decision. Some continued working for him while others left his employment.

I believe Thomas A. Edison, in spite of his extreme work habits, to be one of the most important capitalist in the history of America due to his inventive mind. Perhaps I should not refer to him as a capitalist since he had a high disregard for both capitalists and financial men which almost matched his hatred for mathematicians. He wrote on one of his patents: "Invented by & for myself and not for any small-brained capitalist".[32]

One of the important inventions he produced was the incandescent light bulb. We all realize this invention was one of the most significant of all but it was during those experiments he conducted to perfect the incandescent light bulb that he unwittingly produced a rectifier. A rectifier is used to convert electrical alternating current to direct current. This invention led to the vacuum tube in which the direct current was vital for use in the development of radio.[33]

Another of his accomplishments was to construct the first central electrical power-plant in New York City. Widespread use of electricity in downtown Manhattan was made possible by his collaboration with Louis Tiffany. Together they designed and decorated the first electrically lit theater in the world.[34] There can be no doubt that Thomas A. Edison is responsible for many of the comforts we Americans and the world enjoy as we go through our daily routine of living.

He not only invented many items we use today but he improved upon other people's inventions. One such major achievement pertained to the telephone. Alexander Graham Bell invented the telephone in 1876. The major drawback on his telephone was that it could only operate for a distance of two to three miles. After many experiments on the telephone, Edison improved the device where it could be used over an unlimited distance.[35]

It seemed while Edison would be working on improving another person's invention, he would accidentally discover something which would lead to a new device which was then registered as his invention. He had observed how the phone's diaphragm vibrated in concert with his voice as he spoke. He thought if the vibrations were recorded on a device, the sounds could be preserved and reproduced. A needle was held against the diaphragm to test the strengths of the vibrations as he shouted at different levels. By holding the needle in such a manner as to allow it to prick his finger, he determined the force of the prick varied with the different levels of volume he would shout.

Next he attached a needle to the diaphragm and placed the other end against a piece of waxed paper. He would steadily pull the strip of paper as he would shout the word "hello" several times at different levels of volume. Groves were produced by the needle during this procedure. He then pulled the strip underneath the needle which followed the grooves the needle had previously made. This pushed the needle against the diaphragm which in turn reproduced the shouts Edison had voiced. Thus was born the phonograph which was produced by him at a later time.[36]

To further mention his numerous inventions would take away the intent of this book. However, I feel it is important for us to realize that without the freedom which is found in America, Edison would not have had the inclination to work the way he did. He was willing to work under the same conditions he required of his employees. If the government had been looking over his shoulder and forcing him to file numerous forms to justify his inventions, it can be said with a great deal of certainty that his genius mind would have been stifled. I will admit from a personal perspective, though, it would have been difficult for me to have been one of his employees.

Henry Ford (1863-1941) was born on a farm in Greenfield Township, Michigan. Through his living as a child on the farm, he realized the importance of transportation to aid the farmers to get their produce to the market and for social life among the farmers. This would be instrumental in his drive to provide such transportation in the future. At the age of sixteen, he left the farm and went to Detroit to learn the skill of a machinist. After several years, he returned to the family farm and worked part-time for the Westinghouse Engine Company. Having set up a small machine shop on the family farm when he returned, he began to tinker with engines and machines. He did this for several years before moving back to Detroit where he was made chief engineer at the Detroit Edison Company.[37]

Ford found himself working directly under the tutelage of Thomas Edison. Under this guidance he learned the skills of entrepreneurship and ingenuity in creating products for which there was a market. The hours he worked were irregular which gave him time to experiment with gasoline engines. He successfully built his first gasoline engine in 1892. In Ford's mind, the internal-combustion engine, combined with the cheap gasoline which was already available, would provide a cheap mode of transportation if the vehicle were priced at a level where the ordinary person could afford to purchase it. The first successful vehicle he produced and sold was a Quadricycle which was a buggy frame mounted on four bicycle wheels and powered by a small gasoline motor. This was in 1896. He sold these vehicles to raise capital for future ventures. With capital he raised from Detroit citizens, he formed the Ford Motor Company in 1903. Five years later he introduced the Model T which became a very successful product.[38]

Ford was able to produce the Model T at a cost which permitted him to sell it to the public at a price they could afford. In 1909, Ford Motor Company had sold 10,607 autos. Following a theory which had been developed by Frederick W. Taylor in 1911, Ford put in place a method of mass production of the parts which went into the vehicle. Workers were given the tasks of mass producing the parts needed to build the automobiles by using the motion and time study which Taylor had developed while a steel company foreman. By closely analyzing every job in the mill, he worked out a system of finely detailed division of labor, and piecework wage systems, to increase production and profits.

As a result of implementing the motion and time study system in his plant, Ford sold 198,000 in 1913 and 248,000 in 1914. With personal knowledge of the motion and time study method of costing, it is easy to understand how Ford was able to reduce the $850 price of the Model T in 1908 to $360 in 1916 when he sold 577,036 autos. This was despite increasing his labor costs when he had decided to pay his workers $5 per day thus enabling them to buy the automobiles they built.[39]

The Taylor Motion and Time study was still being taught at the University of Cincinnati in 1956 when I was taking courses in pursuit of my Associate Degree in Factory Management. It provided me with a very valuable tool when I became the Purchasing Manager at my place of employment. Vendor factory visits enabled me to gather information about the manufacturing method of the major product our company used (over 3,000,000 pounds of brass rod/year). The suppliers were very cooperative in providing information concerning the different operations which were required to produce the rod. With further information about the per foot speeds their machinery ran to produce a pound of rod, I was capable of closely determining the labor costs to manufacture the rod. With that information, added to the market price of the raw material cost, it enabled me to purchase the product at a very realistic price per pound. This was information I needed to know to be assured our competitors were not able to purchase the rod at a price level which would put them at a material cost advantage.

Henry Ford was an industrial leader who understood the characteristics of capitalism. One of the problems he had encountered in running his factory was an unstable workforce. At the urging of James Couzens, Ford Motor Vice President and Treasurer, Ford made the decision to increase his workers pay to $5 per day.[40] By investing in higher wages, Ford stopped the tremendous worker turnover he had encountered and, as previously stated, he also turned his workers into consumers of the automobiles they were building. With a more stable workforce, productivity increased which enabled him to reduce the price of the automobile being produced. As any accountant knows, when an increase in units produced occurs, there are more units to be applied against the fixed costs of the factory, thus resulting in a lowering of overall costs.

Ford's action of increasing the workers weekly pay was driven by the profit motive. His profits increased tremendously. Though he had increased his workers pay voluntarily, he remained a staunch conservative who ran his business with the hand of a tyrant. He supposedly fired any of his workers who were caught driving a competitor's automobile. Any effort to unionize the factories were met with hired strike-breaking goons. This resistance toward unions remained until 1941 when he finally relented.

For his creativity of developing the mass production method and concept of increased productivity which aided Americans to be able to afford the automobile, I believe Henry Ford to be one of the greatest industrialists in our history. Due to his intellect, society benefitted unintentionally by having a greater standard of living even though he did not manage his company in a manner to improve society; it just happened. He pulled society forward in the wake of his success in gaining wealth.

America was fortunate to have capitalists which moved this country into an industrialized nation. However, I have written about the different types of capitalists with a question in mind. How much better would our society be today if the business philosophy of Ford had been pursued by those who are known as the Robber Barons?

Chapter 2

Labor Activists in Late 1800s

Striving to overcome their low wages and poor working conditions of the late 1800s, workers attempted to form unions and/or go on strike to bring about changes. Strike breakers, hired by the industrialists to protect what they considered their property rights, used violence to prevent the workers efforts to make changes. During this period, many workers and strike breakers lost their lives as a result of the violence. Labor reformers of this period felt the degradation which had taken place in both the government and social morals were the result of the few wealthy individuals, such as the Robber Barons, who had corrupted government with bribes to appease their quest for vast wealth.

Labor leaders, who wanted to reclaim the moral demeanor of government and industry people, began to speak out about the decadence which had spread throughout America. "We stand as the conservators of society", a Vermont labor leader declared in 1887.[1] Many in the labor movement had no desire to return to the days before the industrial development which had taken place in America. Their goal was to cleanse the government of the corruption which was prevalent throughout all levels. In John Swinton's publication, A Momentous Question: The Respective Attitudes of Labor and Capital, he wrote: "There will soon be but two parties in the field, one composed of honest workingmen, lovers of justice and equality, the other...composed of kid-gloved, silk-stockinged, aristocratic capitalists and their contemptible toadies."[2]

There were many people involved in the effort to improve the working conditions in America. Some felt the way to this goal was through socialism or anarchy, while others sought to seek changes by working within the present confines of industry and government. It is not my intention to identify all the individuals who were involved in the labor movement. Rather, some of the persons mentioned had a small part in seeking to change the economic system in the United

States. Others played a large, direct part in changing the way the workers were being treated by the industrialists.

Lucy Parsons was a woman who is described as a militant anarchist. She was an African-American who insisted she was an orphan who had Mexican and Indian parents. Though she would not acknowledge her actual ancestry, she very strongly denounced Ku Klux Klan rapes and lynches that took place in the Waco, Texas region where she lived in the 1860s. She is, perhaps, best known for her relationship with a man who would become her husband, Albert Parsons.[3]

Parsons was the son of a prominent New England family whose ancestors came to America on the Mayflower. Other Parson ancestors graduated from Harvard and Yale, one was a pastor of an early Congregational church, while others were important military figures in the Revolutionary War. Albert arrived in Waco before the Civil War where he worked as a printer apprentice. When the Civil War broke out, he served in the Confederate Army. After the War ended, the Reconstruction period found him to be a Radical Republican. It was while he was speaking for African-American rights at meetings where he encouraged them to become voters that he gained the confidence of the black community, including Lucy. In 1869, when he and Lucy set-up house, they crossed over the social line which did not allow race mixing. With the failure of Reconstruction in 1873, Lucy and he decided it would be best if they moved into the northern part of America. They settled in Chicago and became active in the political left movement which was starting to emerge in America.[4]

Albert lost his job with a newspaper in Chicago after making speeches during the 1877 railroad strike. This forced Lucy to set up a dress shop which became their sole support. She became obsessively angry about the violent manner the police and militia treated working people. It was then that she reached the conclusion that there could be no reconciliation between labor and capital. She and Albert became widely known in Chicago as radical anarchists. This reputation would eventually lead to the arrest and execution of him following the 1886 Haymarket Square bombing.[5]

The political left was struggling with their differences between socialism and anarchism. Although both viewpoints challenged the idea of private property in America, the differences were very clear. Socialists were advocates of government ownership of the means of production, whereas, the anarchists felt that organized government was by its very nature oppressive. What both lines of thought failed to take into account is that each wanted to be the group which replaced those who were at that time in control of manufacturing and government in America. Why do people who want to take away the freedom of others to accomplish their goals, believe they are more capable of providing an equitable society?

Another person who was considered a radical was Oscar Ameringer. When he arrived in Cincinnati in 1886, there were violent class conflicts throughout America. He found the skills of cabinet-making and playing musical instruments which had been taught him by his father in Germany were meaningless in the furniture factories where he sought employment. He became very dissatisfied with a job he acquired because he had to perform ten hours of boring work for only one dollar a day. When the May Day strikes, which were led by socialist in the labor movement, came to Cincinnati in 1886, Ameringer quit his job and joined the Lehr and Wehr-Venn. To educate and protect the German workers, this organization had formed a labor battalion which had four hundred of their members who were armed with Springfield rifles.[6]

Eventually, 32,000 Cincinnati workers became part of the May strikes. Following the ending of the strikes most of the workers found their way back to their jobs. Ameringer was unable to return to his job because he was blacklisted for assaulting a strikebreaker outside the furniture factory where he had been employed. A disillusioned Ameringer became very active in Cincinnati's German-American socialist community where he spent his remaining years as a writer and agitator.[7]

Ameringer looked upon socialism as a cause where the government would own the mines and factories. This would preserve the workers' dignity and right to a livelihood.[7] Though his vision was utopian in nature, he failed to take into account that some people are prone to work diligently while others' work habits are at a lesser pace. This personality difference creates problems among the workers as the tasks of production are performed.

The efforts of the socialists and anarchists to form unions to support their strategy to improve the working and wage conditions in America failed. Many of the workers, though they were unsatisfied with the wages and working conditions of their work place, were content with the freedoms they had found in America. They did not wish to see those freedoms lost as a result of a socialist government or no government at all. At least in a capitalistic system, society could seek to correct any injustices by dealing directly with the capitalists who create the jobs.

The period from 1876 to 1886 showed a tremendous growth in organized labor unions which had preservation of freedoms as one of their goals. Among the first group of laborers to form unions were the skilled craftsmen in the building trades, foundries and small consumer-goods industries.[8] One of the groups to become organized were nine Philadelphia tailors. They organized as the Noble and Holy Order of the Knights of Labor in 1869 under a cloak of secrecy. This secrecy was felt to be necessary because the companies used firing and blacklisting of workers to undercut unionism. Because of the failed railroad strikes in 1877, the question of secrecy was challenged,. The leaders of the Knights realized the tremendous reach and power of national corporations made it necessary for working people to be organized as open and public labor organizations on a national level to do battle with the forces of capital.[9]

In 1879, the Knights chose Terence V. Powderly as the Grand Master Workman who would lead the Knights of Labor for the next fifteen years. Powderly brought the Knights a leadership view of a deep belief in temperance, education and land reform. He was also inclined to do away with the wage system which was currently in place. With him as it's leader, the secrecy of the Knights was gradually eliminated.[10] Membership in the Knights of Labor was opened to everyone. Local assemblies offered all workers, whether they were black or white, male or female, a means to counter the offers of individual advancement to workers which the capitalists promised.[11]

The Knights felt their organization was good for America. They believed the monopolies, the corruption in politics, and the overzealous competition as having a negative impact on America. It became their goal to save what they felt was positive in the republican tradition. To accomplish this, they wanted to eliminate the political corruption and industrial degradation which they felt was destroying the freedom of the American people.[12]

There were some persons who became involved in the labor movement for their personal gain. One such individual was Patrick Henry McCarthy whose view of a better way of life for the worker was to mix trade-union militancy and rejecting socialism by committing to political accommodation. Having been born in Ireland in 1863, he moved to America in 1880 to work as a carpenter's apprentice. In 1886, he arrived in San Francisco where he was involved with the beginning of the Brotherhood of Carpenters and Joiners in the late 1880s. From that position, he was involved in organizing the city's powerful Building Trades Council in 1898. He ruled the Council for twenty four years.[13]

Strong trade union powers was a way of life in San Francisco in 1886. With it being located on the west coast of America, more work was available than the building tradesmen could accomplish. Tight control over who could work on construction sites assured jobs for the building tradesmen who belonged to the union. Union cards were required in order to work, the union workers followed the rule of sharing employment with other union workers by "informally" restricting their output so there would be enough work to go around. With these restrictions came good wages for all the union workers. The Building Trades Council became a union which was interested in their workers plight but was not concerned about the conditions under which the non-union workers were forced to work. Admission to the union was usually limited to the sons of present members and no African-Americans need apply for membership.

McCarthy, as the union leader, was a benefactor of such a policy. He became very wealthy and soon adopted the persona of a "responsible pillar of the community". The strong economic and political power displayed by the skilled workers of the union indicated their interests were in class rather than in individual terms.[14] This is an example of how the labor movement began to become self-centered among separate union groups and non-union worker groups which would, later in history, create problems for the union.

One of the giants in the labor movement in America was Samuel Gompers (1850-1924) who was born in London where his father was a cigar maker. He had to quit school when he was ten years old to help support the family by working as an apprentice shoemaker. It was not long before he decided that trade was not for him so he took up the trade of cigar making with his father. More money was needed to support the family so his father began to think about taking his family to America. At that time, 1863, the United States was involved with the Civil War. Most of the workers in England were sympathetic towards the Union's views concerning slavery. The Gompers family migrated to America in 1863 and settled in New York City where they lived in an apartment located in the Lower East Side.

Samuel and his father had no trouble finding work as cigar rollers in one of the cigar shops. It didn't take long for Samuel to gain recognition as a skilled cigar roller by his employer. Likewise, his personification was such that his fellow workers recognized that he was an aggressive and confident spokesman for them. With that recognition, he was elected president of his local union, CMU 144 in 1875. A plan of action was formed by Gompers of which the first task was to revitalize the Cigarmakers' Union. Under Gompers leadership, the organization of the union was tightened, dues were raised, and a clear, limited agenda was developed by Gompers, (Chasen, 1971 & Kaufman, 1973).[15]

The Cigar Makers sent Gompers to a conference of various unions. At that conference, a loose confederation was formed which was named the Federation of Organized Trades and Labor unions of the United States and Canada (FOTLU). It began as an annual congress of national unions and local labor councils with the focus of the organization to be educating the public concerning working-class issues. It was also to prepare labor legislation, and lobby the U.S. Congress to act on such legislation. (Salvatore, 1984).[16]

It became apparent to Gompers that the new organization had neither the money nor the authority to do more than just talk about the issues. In 1886, he helped found the American Federation of Labor. The first elected president of the American Federation of Labor (AFL) was Samuel Gompers. He served as it's president every year for the rest of his life except for the year of 1895 when he was ousted by a socialist movement to take over the organization.[17]

One of Gompers' goals was to see the workers receive a greater share of the wealth being created by their work efforts. He was not interested in the concept of improving society as a whole, therefore, he was uninterested in organizing for political reasons. The American Federation of Labor's growth from 150,000 in 1886 to over one million members in 1901 indicated the American workers shared these views.[18] The viewpoints which Patrick Henry McCarthy and Samuel Gompers presented became the predominate approach used in labor's pursuit for better wages and improved working conditions. Labor union membership continued to grow until 1920 when it reached 5 million workers.

Chapter 3

Violent Conflicts in Late 1880s

In their effort to improve wages and working conditions by forming unions, the workers encountered determined capitalists who felt their companies were constitutionally protected as private property rights. This view was challenged by Henry George (1839-1897), a printer and newspaperman who, as a young man, had gone to Calcutta, India while he was a seaman aboard a ship. It was there he saw the enormous spread between the wealthy and poor of that country. He produced a book entitled Progress and Poverty (1879) in which he wrote that the existence of great wealth and extreme poverty was caused by the prevalent view that individuals who owned land were entitled to the production of other's labor and had absolute rights.[1]

In his book, A History of the American People, Paul Johnson writes that George was correct to challenge that prevailing view. Henry George concluded that progress would be a continuing process to better human rights inasmuch as the right to ownership of land would prevail. However, such rights were a trust which should be discharged with responsibility. George felt if the owners of land did not consider it their responsibility to be concerned about social justice, then the government should urge them to reconsider. Failure by the owners to reconsider their viewpoint, it was his opinion that the state should then force them in the right direction by legislative means. This was the only alternative to counter the demands for outright socialism according to George.[2] The American capitalists, at that time, rejected the view expressed by George. This led them to oppose attempts by others to interfere with the running of their business since they considered it to be their property rights. As time passed, the capitalists, determined to resist any outside interference, decided to meet such opposition by any means, including physical methods, should it become necessary.

The Knights of Labor had increased in stature by 1886 when they decided to become active in the political scene. In Rutland, Vermont the United Labor Party was capable of electing a Knights of Labor candidate to the state legislature in that year's election. They also succeeded in electing their fifteen justice of peace candidates to office.[3] This success led the Knights to overestimate their strength. During a strike which had been approved by them, the employers refused to willingly negotiate in 1886-87 even though they had done so in 1884-85.

Capitalists began to use their trade associations as a means to counter the activities of labor by locking out those workers who had joined the unions. These same capitalists began using the government to conduct legal but threatening acts against the unions. The striking workers were subjected to legal charges such as inciting to riot, obstructing the streets and trespassing. By this action of the capitalists, the Knights realized their strength had subsided within the present environment. The fact that management decided it was no longer necessary to cater to workers demands convinced the Knights, on May 4, 1886 to call off the strike they had authorized.

It was inevitable that people who had strong feelings concerning the two opposite viewpoints would become involved in violent acts at different places in America. One such event took place in Chicago. The labor unions were determined to have an eight-hour work day recognized by management. The political radicals such as Albert Parsons, August Spies, Michael Schwab and Samuel Fielden were responsible for agitating the workers towards violence while they were making the eight-hour work day demand. On May 1, 1886, an estimated 40,000 workers struck in an attempt to accomplish their goal. A parade of 80,000 was led by Anarchist Albert Parsons and August Spies. The parade that day was peaceful. However, that was the calm before the storm. On May 3, during a bloody fight between strikers and scabs at the McCormick Reaper Works, the police were called in to quell the violence. Many people were beaten by the police and before it was over, two workers were shot and killed. August Spies was there to witness the beatings and killings. He printed a bulletin and distributed it urging the workers to assemble for a protest rally at Haymarket Square on the evening of May 4, 1886.[4]

Poor weather and the sudden call for the rally to be held the next day was responsible for a small crowd to be present. With the threat of rain, the already small crowd became even smaller as workers left to escape any foul weather. Samuel Fielden began to speak to the approximately 300 people remaining. Before he finished speaking, the police moved in to break up the rally. When that occurred, someone in the crowd threw a bomb which killed one policeman. The police became enraged, losing control of their emotions and began acting like a mob out of control. They opened fire upon the crowd with their guns, killing one and wounding many more including policemen. A Chicago Herald reporter wrote about what happened and called it a scene of "wild carnage".[5] This incident of violence was not necessarily aimed directly at the capitalists as much as it was an attempt to overthrow the economic system of capitalism in America. The political views of Parsons and his fellow anarchists were very prevalent throughout the entire Haymarket Square demonstration.

The Chicago Press, by the manner in which they wrote about the event, caused the Chicago civic leaders to embark upon an anti-radical anti-immigrant campaign to seek revenge for the killing of the policeman. Eight anarchist leaders, including Parsons and Spies, were quickly arrested. They were charged with conspiracy to commit murder. Following a trial in which they were convicted, each was sentenced to be executed. They were found guilty despite the fact that no evidence was presented which would have connected them to the unidentified bomb thrower. Parsons, Spies and two of their comrades were executed in November 1887.[6]

Capitalists continued to grow bolder in their actions toward labor. During the second half of 1886, 100,000 workers were locked out of their jobs. The declining ability of the Knights of Labor to protect its members workplace rights became evident with the harsh defeats suffered by the laundry workers in Troy, New York, the packing-house workers in Chicago, and the knitters in Cohoes and Amsterdam, New York. These defeats cost the Knights a great deal of dues paying members. In 1886, they had claimed 1,000,000 supporters. That number fell to 500,000 one year later and by 1890, the membership was only 100,000.[7]

Another act of violence occurred in 1892 at the Carnegie Homestead Works steel mill in Homestead, Pennsylvania just outside of Pittsburgh. Carnegie had made many wage concessions to the skilled workers who were represented by the Amalgamated Association during the 1870s and 1880s. However, it was in 1889 that Carnegie made a concession which he regretted. To end the strike he had granted a wage increase to the skilled workers which put their wages one-third higher than other steel mills in the area. In addition to the wage increase to the skilled workers, the wages of the unskilled workers were tied to the skilled workers. That meant that whenever a wage increase was granted to the skilled workers, the unskilled workers also received a wage increase. The workers of Homestead shared common interests. To them unionism was a right of citizenship. It is said that a state militia officer remarked, "They believe the works is quite as much theirs as it is Carnegie's".[8]

In the early part of 1892, Carnegie reevaluated his workforce and decided he wanted a cheaper and more docile labor force. He opined the Amalgamated Association would prevent him from accomplishing such a goal. It was on this issue that the previously stated views which had been instilled in him by his father and mother created a personal clash within him. His desire to be frugal conflicted with his view about fairness to his workers. Not having the desire to confront these two views within himself, he told his associate Henry Clay Frick what he wanted to accomplish and left for Scotland on an extended vacation. The task of confronting the Association, which meant breaking the union, was left up to Frick.[9]

It was during June of 1892 that Frick began to set his plan in place. The first step he took was to inform the workers that henceforth he would deal with them on an individual basis only. Next he informed the union that he would not be renewing the contract with Amalgamated Association. Accepting the fact that the union would not agree to those conditions, Frick knew he would have to do something to prevent the union from shutting down steel production at the Homestead Works. Any work stoppage would have to be on his terms.[10]

The initial strategy was to place a three mile, 12 feet high, fence around the perimeter of the mill. Placing barbed wire on top of the fence made him feel secure that no one could climb the fence to create a problem in the mill. To provide protection for the scab workers he was planning on bringing in to operate the mill he hired three hundred

Pinkerton agents. Frick's plan was to bring the workers down the river and unload them directly onto the company property. With his plan ready to be activated, he shut down the Homestead Works on July 2, 1892 and announced he would reopen it with non-union workers.[11]

The union workers of Homestead Works were not going to stand by and let Frick's plan succeed without putting up a fight. Some of the workers and other town members took control of all the utilities. Others patrolled all the land, water, and rail means of access to Homestead. On July 5, armed men hired by Pinkerton and non-union workers approached the mills on a barge. They felt confident about their mission of unloading the scabs on the plant property. Unbeknownst to the armed Pinkerton men, the union workers, their families and other town people had been made known of their strategy and were waiting on the river bank when the barge arrived. They were armed with guns and also had a small cannon. A battle took place for twelve hours, during which nine strikers and seven Pinkerton detectives were killed and numerous others on both sides were wounded. The Pinkertons finally decided it would be best for them to surrender to the strikers and stop the bloodshed.[12]

Upon hearing the results of the day, Frick contacted the governor's office for help. The governor was reluctant to intervene but upon learning more about the situation, he decided to send in the state militia. When the militia arrived, a spokesman for the union greeted them with the statement: "On the part of the Amalgamated Association, I wish to say that after suffering an attack of illegal authority, we are glad to have the legal authority of the state here." The General in command of the troops was less gracious: "I do not recognize your association, sir...we have come here to restore law and order."[13]

Law and order became difficult for the militia to achieve, though. It was necessary for them to escort the strikebreakers into all of the Carnegie plants because of continued violence by the members of the union. When the union workers who had been arrested were brought to trial, the juries would find them not guilty. This scenario continued until November 18 when the unskilled workers finally appealed to the union to end their strike. Amalgamated Association accepted their appeal and called off the strike. The leaders of the union were fired and blacklisted. Frick sent a wire to Carnegie telling him the strike had ended and declared there would be no future trouble from the workers.

With the end of the strike, the union was in a weakened condition. They realized the past power of their union was dramatically reduced. Carnegie had won because of the power he held as the owner. Government had intervened upon his behalf when the workers resorted to violence while attempting to protect their jobs. Sadly, lives were lost in that struggle because of the hardened positions by both capitalists and labor. The time for level headed thinking had not yet arrived. I mention these violent confrontations to remind people of the deadly struggles in the attempt to control capitalism. Deaths on both sides were unnecessary. Why did it have to escalate to such a level? Labor/capital relationships had a long way to go as both sides felt they were right in the battle to control capitalism.

Labor unions are part of a good and free capitalistic economic system. It is because of the influence the unions exert that the capitalists involuntarily grant workers a greater share of the wealth they produce. Only through union influences are working conditions improved by capitalists as far as safety and cleanliness are concerned.

Workers in non-union companies benefit from union's influence in labor/capital relations. Employers not desiring a unionized work force usually keep their companies abreast of the union-labor wages and union-plant work environment to make it unnecessary for their employees to consider forming a union to improve their wage and work conditions. Union members and their leaders must understand, however, that there is a limit placed upon their demands by the marketplace into which their employer sells their product or service. Too great a demand can bring about job loss and/or inflation due to higher productivity costs.

A willingness by both the employers and employees to sit down and discuss the issues of employment should be conducted with a "team" approach. There should be no loser in such discussions. Those who feel they have "lost" will allow the feeling to fester until it explodes sometime in the future. After all, emotional feelings are a common thread in all of us. The episode at the Homestead Works was a perfect example of both sides unwilling to understand this concept of cooperative negotiation.

Carnegie had become too self-centered in the management of his company. There is no indication that the company had become unprofitable or that worker complacency had set in. When workers are made to feel they are part of the company's future, they will not tolerate complacency by the workforce. The episode at the Homestead Works was a perfect example of both sides unwilling to understand this concept of cooperative negotiation. As a result of this incident, the quest for controlled capitalism was set back. A "battlefield approach" in labor/capital relationships would prevail for many years.

Chapter 4

Struggles to Control Capitalism

Newspaper and magazine editors, in the late 1800s, began to write about the conditions in which many of the workers in America were forced to work and live. They published articles about the corruption in the political and business segments of American life. These publications were followed by a loud outcry of public opinion against such abhorrent practices. Even in those days, the politicians listened to that outcry and began to clean up their act. Consequently, in 1890, Congress passed the Sherman Antitrust Act. The main thrust of this legislation was to limit the concentration of power which interfered with trade and reduced economic competition. Another provision of the Act made it illegal to monopolize any part of trade or commerce in the United States.

Little was accomplished by the Justice Department as they attempted to enforce the law against corporations because of narrow interpretations by the judicial system of what constituted trade or commerce among states. The most effective use of the Act was against unions. They were considered to be illegal combinations in the rulings handed down by the courts, thus limiting their activities. It would be many years before a presidential administration would use it's power to breakup the Trusts which had been established by the wealth individuals.

The voice of the Populists Party, a political party which was found by the Grangers and the few remaining members of the Knights of Labor during a convention in St. Louis in 1892, began to be heard. They spoke out boldly about the corruption in government and the political parties but their voice did not resonate with the American people in the way of national votes. Though the votes did not materialize from their rhetoric, it did provoke discussions about their platform. That platform called "for national ownership of railroads and telegraph and telephone systems, a system of keeping nonperishable crops off the market, and a graduated income tax".[1]

Their platform was an eloquent indictment of the times: "We meet in the midst of a nation brought to the verge of moral, political, and material ruin. Corruption dominates the ballot-box, the Legislatures, the Congress, and touches even the ermine of the bench. The people are demoralized...the newspapers are largely subsidized or muzzled, public opinion silenced...the fruits of the toil of millions are boldly stolen to build up colossal fortunes for a few...from the same prolific womb of governmental injustice we breed the two great classes - tramps and millionaires." The men in power did not watch idly. In the South, Democrats undermined the Populist organizing effort by heightening racial fears. The mass of urban workers were never drawn to Populism, preferring to deal with the Democrat machines that they thought were defending their interests.[2]

With capitalism still uncontrolled, a severe depression brought on by the Panic of 1893 created problems within America. The "laws of economics" had brought about a society in chaos. The financial world had collapsed when 500 banks failed and 16,000 businesses were forced to close due to bankruptcy. The "laws of economics" creates a cleansing of the poorly managed companies within any economic system, whether it be socialism, communism or capitalism. The cleansing takes place much quicker in capitalism with a more efficient recovery than socialism and communism systems. Bureaucracy in socialism and communism prevents swift cleansing, thus allowing poorly managed companies to exist for longer periods. In capitalism, entrepreneurs make decisions to enhance the operations of their company without having to rely on government bureaucrats to change or improve their method of operations. Little or no involvement of the government, however, will lead to the swing of the symbolic pendulum of the "laws of economics" to the extreme right or extreme left. The results are "booms" and "busts" in the economy. The negatives of these two extremes are the inflation caused by the "booms" and the extreme hardships on people which is caused by the "busts". There must be an attempt to control these wide economic swings.

When 150 railroads went into bankruptcy, other industries such as steel companies and other companies which did business with the steel companies also were forced into bankruptcy. The Depression which was caused by the 1893 Panic lasted five years. It was the first time the new industrial society in America faced such a severe downturn in the economy. Having never faced such a colossal financial catastrophe, the American people did not know what to do. Millions of people had no income. Some people who were homeless were provided shelter in jails. Starvation was something which threatened the lives of millions. At the 1893 convention of the American Federation of Labor, they declared that "the right to work is the right to live" and called for an eight-hour day to spread what work there was available among an increased number of workers. They also advocated that the federal government issue $500 million in paper money to fund public works.[3]

The mayor of Detroit designated empty lots where unemployed workers were permitted to grow vegetables. The idea spread to several other cities where such a project helped to provide much needed food. With the economy in such a dire strait, though, this effort didn't come close to meeting the need among the poor and unemployed.

A person would have thought a great swell of compassion would have come forth from the rich and those who were fortunate to have jobs. It did not. In fact, some of the people who normally were involved in helping the needy felt that providing a handout to the unemployed was wrong. They believed such aid would lead to socialism. Instead of granting government aid to those in need, one opinion expressed was that the unemployed should be given jobs which were hard and underpaid. The reasoning behind such a viewpoint was that if a person hates their job because it is too hard or the pay is not enough to live on they will do everything in their power to get a better job. Unfortunately, during the 1893 Depression there was no job available for the unemployed.

As in any situation where people are desperate, the unemployed workers struck out against anyone who considered themselves superior to them. At the same time when there was high unemployment, strikes were occurring throughout America. It was difficult to understand such a scenario. To help alleviate the problem of high unemployment, an Ohio businessman, Jacob S. Coxey, presented a plan to Congress which would put thousands of unemployed back to work. He recommended using them to improve the roads in America. It upset him when Congress turned a cool head to the plan.[4]

To show his contempt for the way Congress rejected his plan, Coxey called for a march on Washington by the unemployed workers to press Congress to enact his plan. Much to his disillusionment only a hundred people showed up to begin the march. He had expected there to be thousands. By the time they arrived at Homestead, Pennsylvania, six hundred more had joined the marchers. They became more encouraged as they marched through other industrial communities. Thousands lined the streets and cheered them on the way to Washington. This march differed from the many marches to Washington which had taken place in previous years. These marchers were appealing "to the federal government for relief, asserting that the federal government had a basic responsibility for the people's welfare." They attempted to change the phrase "life, liberty and the pursuit of happiness" to "life, liberty and the means of happiness."[4]

President Grover Cleveland, who had been re-elected in 1892 after having been defeated by Benjamin Harrison in 1888, refused to recognize the new interpretation and sent word that he would enforce a law which prohibited parades on the Capitol grounds. On May 1, 1894, the marchers reached Washington. They were met by a huge police force which immediately arrested Coxey and the other leaders. A riot broke out which was quickly quelled. The rest of the marchers quietly disbanded and went home.

Theodore Roosevelt (1858-1919) was born in New York to a family which was wealthy and prominent in society. As a child he had a very sickly life which was caused by severe asthma attacks. He became determined to overcome his condition by making his body strong which he accomplished through strenuous exercise. His mind was keen which helped to develop a character of honesty and fairness. From the first time he entered into the political arena with the Republican party in New York, he was a strong advocate of reform in government and business practices. During the three terms he served in the New York Assembly, he garnered a reputation as a reformer with integrity by being outspoken and an active opponent against those whom he referred to as the wealthy criminal class of America.

During the 1884 presidential election, Roosevelt experienced a setback in his political career. As a delegate to the national Republican convention, he strongly supported Senator George F. Edmunds for president. This support was in opposition to James G. Blaine whom Roosevelt felt was not an honest individual. When Blaine won the nomination, Roosevelt had a difficult decision to make. He could refuse to support Blaine along with the other progressives in the party or he could support Blaine and hope for an appointment should he be elected. With the defeat of Blaine, Roosevelt did not receive any appointment and it appeared his political career was over. However, as history records, the defeat was not permanent.

In 1888, Roosevelt saw the opportunity to get back into the political arena and campaigned for Benjamin Harrison. When Harrison was elected, he was appointed to be a Civil Service Commissioner. He knew the Civil Service was corrupt and worked diligently to clean it up and make the work it performed more accommodating to the public. The appointment, along with the later appointment to Police Commissioner of New York, enabled him to sustain his reputation as an effective reformer with integrity.

When the Democrats nominated William Jennings Bryan as their presidential candidate in 1896, Mark Hanna, an Ohio industrial giant and wealthy individual, provided much of the financial resources needed to have William McKinley, governor of Ohio, nominated on the Republican ticket. During the campaign, the Republicans outspent the Democrats by an overwhelming 25 to 1 ratio which resulted in the election of McKinley. In 1897, he appointed Theodore Roosevelt to be his Assistant Secretary of Navy. Little did America realize then that he would become the future president who would take on the powerful industrialists and bankers.

Roosevelt was a strong advocate for the preparation of a war with Spain while serving as Assistant Secretary of Navy. When war was declared, he resigned the position and formed a cavalry unit which became known as the Rough Riders. They went to Cuba where Roosevelt gained national notoriety as the leader of the heroic charge up San Juan Hill. Upon his return to America, he was greeted with enthusiasm by the Republican Party in New York. They urged him to seek the office of governor in New York which he won by a small margin. Thomas C. Platt, the New York Republican boss, had supported Roosevelt during the campaign.

After he had been inaugurated, Roosevelt imposed taxes on utility franchises. This did not meet with the approval of Platt as he had assured the public utility corporations that the policy of them not paying taxes would continue. For that reason, and with the help of Thomas Collier, the national Republican Party boss, it was decided to "kick him upstairs" by arranging for his nomination as McKinley's vice-presidential running mate in 1900. They never gave a thought that Roosevelt would be just a heartbeat away from the presidency should McKinley be elected. Such an event occurred when President McKinley was shot on September 6, 1901 and died on September 14, 1901 at which time Theodore Roosevelt became the twenty-sixth President of the United States.

The newspapers and magazines in America were very effective during the 1880-90s in pointing out the anti-social excesses of capitalism. Many investigative stories were written about the wrong doing of the bankers and industrialists who used their power and money to corrupt the branches of state and federal governments. The news media disclosed many of the corrupt business activities these same individuals practiced. Roosevelt had been aware of the wrong doings and decided to take aim at correcting such anti-social activities when he became President in 1901.[5]

By this time, a strong middle-class had developed in America. They were educated and aware of the corruption that was prevalent in America. Therefore, they were willing to support any effort by President Theodore Roosevelt in his drive to clean up the evil doings of the bankers and industrialists. Roosevelt believed it was proper for the government to make sure business was responsive to the needs of the public. He felt that a monopoly was a good thing but it had to be regulated. In his mind, bigness actually led to economic benefits in business such as increased productivity and efficiency. It was his belief, though, that all the Trusts which had been formed by such people as J.P. Morgan and John D. Rockefeller were in violation of the Sherman Anti-Trust Act which had been passed in 1890 but had never been used to prosecute Trusts. Only unions had been prosecuted under the Act which restrained their activities. Many of the people with progressive views felt the Trusts were wrong and wanted to see all of them discontinued. Roosevelt, however, felt there were good Trusts and bad Trusts. Some Trusts were actually serving the public in a proper manner and he wanted to allow them to continue.

On February 18, 1902, Roosevelt asked the Justice Department to prosecute the Northern Securities Company, which was under the control of J.P. Morgan, by using the Sherman Anti-Trust Act as their guide. This Trust had been set up by Morgan to control many of the powerful railroad companies. During Roosevelt's administration, there were over forty suits filed against Trusts so the businessmen in America knew he was serious in his efforts to bring the evils of capitalism under control.

Arthur M. Schlesinger, Jr., in his book The Almanac of American History writes about the events related to the United Mine Workers attempt to be recognized by the mine owners in 1902. On May 12, 1902, 140,000 United Mine Workers walked off their jobs and declared they were on strike. John Mitchell, the leader of the workers, stated he would be willing to arbitrate the differences but the owners refused. Most of the mines are owned by the railroad companies which had eliminated all competition. Their policy of selective rebates, and high freight charges caused untold regional hardships. The low paid miners had many grievances such as being forced to live in company houses and pay the company's rental rates. They also are required to buy their supplies with scrip wages from the company stores thus making them feel they are economic slaves.[6]

The owners continue to be stubborn and refuse to recognize the UMW as well as refusing to negotiate with them. The strike continued into October. By that time, the citizenry of the Northeast had become disturbed when the price of coal had risen from $5 to $30 a ton. The owners decided the government will intervene at some time and will demand an end to the strike. They expect the government to support their position as it has in many of the major strikes in the past. On July 17 George F. Baer, President of the Reading Coal and Iron Company, expressed the owners position by stating in a speech, 'The rights and interests of the laboring man will be protected and cared for, not by labor agitators, but by the Christian men to whom God in His infinite wisdom has given the control of the property interests of His country, and upon the successful management of which so much depends."[6] Although the strike is more peaceful than usual, violence occasionally erupts.

Roosevelt knew he did not have constitutional authority to intervene in the strike. With the price of coal increasing, the public began to apply considerable pressure upon him to settle the strike. Proceeding with care, he requested the opposing adversaries to come to the White House for deliberations. The owners showed their contempt by leaving the deliberations in anger. A disappointed Roosevelt arranged to have the Army take over the mines and run them in the "public interests". Sensing that Roosevelt was serious about ending the strike, J. P. Morgan submitted to negotiations. He first met with Secretary of War Elihu Root. On October 16 a Commission of Arbitration was formed. It would be their responsibility to investigate the miners grievances.[6]

While the investigation is ongoing, the miners agreed to return to work. In March 1903 the Commission recommended the owners reconsider their positions on most of the demands for which the miners walkout had begun. The Commission's also recommended that a permanent board of arbitration be formed as well as a token recognition of the worker's union. Higher wages, shorter hours and greater independence from the owners were also part of the recommendation.[6] This brought an end to the confrontation.

The presentation of the events related to the coal mine incident in 1902 exemplifies the reputation which Roosevelt enjoyed. He was a forceful individual and his famous quotation, "speak softly but carry a big stick" illustrated his philosophy about government's ability to become active in fighting against abuses of capitalism. Though he rarely spoke softly, the slogan spoke for itself. Rather than allow the economy to be crippled due to the lack of coal, Roosevelt had put the power of the federal government to work to bring about a solution to the problem.

The United Mine Workers of America (UMWA) had been founded in 1890 with the support of the many Knights of Labor assemblies which were located in the coal mining areas. The mine workers union agreed with the Knight's concept of being an inclusive labor organization. From the founding of the union, the UMWA had sought to build interracial unions throughout the mining regions of West Virginia, Alabama, and Ohio. An African-American from Ohio by the name of Richard L. Davis was elected to the executive board. He traveled throughout the area to bring other black miners into the union.[7]

It was through the efforts of Davis that the black mineworkers joined with the white mineworkers and formed many local unions. The harmony among the black and white mineworkers helped make the UMWA one of the strongest unions in America. African-American mineworkers were supportive of the union activities because of the equal manner in which they were treated within the organization. That attitude within their union enabled the miners to remain inclusive. The strength shown by the UMWA and the approval of the federal government enabled the workers to have a greater say in their work environment.

Unfortunately, at this time in history when unions were gaining success in their efforts to improve conditions within the American workplace, thousands of workers who were of African ancestry were left behind. This was the reason many black workers in the future commented that unions had done nothing to help them gain more fruitful jobs. Without the support of the union's powers, they were left to fend for themselves in menial jobs offered by employers throughout all of America. It would have been much better for the future of America if they had been included in the effort to control capitalism in America.

Theodore Roosevelt led a governmental attempt to remove some of the evils in the capitalistic system of America. The breakup in 1907 of Standard Oil was considered one of his most successful attempts to achieve his goal. His action meant the breakup of a company which had gained a monopolistic control of the nation's oil. Though many of the suits against Trusts were dropped after corporate leaders visited the White House, the message that Roosevelt had sent was that the federal government possessed the power to regulate the way in which corporations conducted their business. They realized that no company was beyond the laws of the land.[8]

Upton Sinclair, a Socialist writer, wrote a novel entitled The Jungle in 1906. The novel exposed the unhealthy conditions within the meat-packing industry. McClure's magazine wrote several articles exposing fraud in patent medicines. The public responded to the writings by demanding something be done about such outrageous activities in the meat and drug industries. The outcry led to the enactment of the Pure Food and Drug Act and the Meat Inspection Act.[9] With these two Acts, Congress was showing the public they understood their desire for safety in the food and drug purchases they made. This demonstrated the differing views between Socialists and the majority of Americans who believed in capitalism. Instead of having the government in charge of production, the people of America desired to establish government rules by which the capitalists must operate. Slowly, but with certainty, the effort to control capitalism was making progress.

Congress approved the Federal Reserve Act in 1913 which gave the public a limited amount of control over the banking industry. This meant the bankers had to cooperate with the government to perform their responsibility of providing a sound banking system in America. The bankers soon began to use the federal regulations imposed upon the banks in a manner which was beneficial to them. Shortly thereafter the bankers were able to attain a majority role on the boards of the regional Federal Reserve Banks. This gave them the ability to control the policies of the Federal Reserve Board. The nation's currency and the credit systems were regulated by the Banks and the Board. In time, other industries influenced the boards and commissions through their leaders to submit regulations for their businesses. The businessmen used the regulations which were approved during this period as a means to bring about orderly markets and decreasing levels of competition.[10]

The Supreme Court limited the use of boycotts in 1908 by stating that the Sherman Antitrust Act prohibited unions and companies alike from restraining interstate commerce by using such tactics. When this ruling was made, the AFL changed their view about not being involved in politics. Samuel Gompers rejected the Socialists plan for independent political action in the labor movement. If their plan had been adopted, the Socialist Party would have become stronger. Not being an advocate for socialism, Gompers, as the leader of the AFL, attempted to persuade both the Republican and Democrat Parties to support labor issues which had been expressed by the union leaders. The Democrats showed more support for the labor issues presented than the Republicans. As a result of their support, the AFL became affiliated with the Democratic Party.

Theodore Roosevelt and William H. Taft became close friends after the assassination of McKinley. Because of the friendship and political closeness, Roosevelt chose Taft to be his successor in the election of 1908. Over the next four years, Roosevelt became disenchanted with Taft and decided to seek the Republican nomination for President in 1912. In The Almanac of American History, Schlesinger indicates the reason behind Roosevelt's disenchantment with Taft was Taft's inability to continue the progressive programs he had begun in his presidency. Taft often failed to mediate the differences between the conservative and liberal wings of the Republican Party. Nonetheless, during Taft's administration much Trust busting as well as some vital legislation was accomplished. Establishing the parcel post system and guiding the constitutional amendments for popular election of senators and a federal income tax through congress was accomplished during the Taft administration.[11]

When the 1912 Republican convention met, the conservatives united and nominated Taft to again be their standard bearer. Roosevelt and others decided to form the Progressive Party and run against Taft, Woodrow Wilson (Democrat's candidate) and Eugene Debs (Socialist's candidate). President Taft was hurt by the split within the Republican Party and lost to Woodrow Wilson in a four way campaign. Wilson was elected President when he garnered 435 electoral votes to Roosevelt's 88 and Taft's 8. Wilson had received much of the middle-class votes who sought reform and also received the support of the AFL.[12]

In his inaugural speech, Wilson said, "The great government we loved has too often been made use of for private and selfish purposes, and those who used it had forgotten the people...Our cry has been 'Let every man look out for himself, let every generation look out for itself, while we reared giant machinery which made it impossible that any but those who stood at the levers of control should have a chance to look out for themselves.'[13] Thus Wilson stated his belief in the interests of labor.

In 1914, Wilson rewarded labor for their support by backing the Clayton Act which was needed to clarify and supplement the Sherman Antitrust Act of 1890. The Clayton Act restricted the use of court injunctions, which had been used against labor to impede their efforts for a more just labor environment. In addition, it made legal the use of peaceful strikes, picketing and boycotts. Though it was strong legislation when passed, it became weakened in the portion pertaining to labor during subsequent judicial decisions. Wilson advocated an eight-hour workday for the railroad workers and a law regulating federal child labor. The Adamson Bill, signed by Wilson, provided for an eight-hour day and time and a half for overtime. Congress passed the Keating-Owen Act which barred from interstate commerce any item made by child labor. When these two items became law, it marked the first time that the federal government showed interest in regulating the conditions under which labor would be required to work.[14]

During his terms in office, Theodore Roosevelt had begun to introduce more federal power into the executive branch of government. A more active government could help eliminate some of the economic and social problems which were created by capitalism. The working people of America had accepted the presence of socialists, radicals, and feminists in their movement of seeking a more equitable society in which to live.[15] It had been this coalition which had helped to elect Woodrow Wilson. In response, he continued the precedent begun by Theodore Roosevelt and the trend continued for many decades. America was making an earnest attempt to bring the iniquities of capitalism under control.

The one group of people who did not benefit during this period when Wilson was attempting to continue the Progressive's plan for a more equal and free society were the African-Americans. The federal government ignored the lynchings which were occurring in the southern part of America. While the African-Americans had made modest economic gains through the political process of the progressive activists, those gains were wiped out by laws which disfranchised them. Wilson's Democrat administration brought on further disfranchisement by removing blacks from federal jobs.[16] It would be several decades before African-Americans would again benefit from government policies. This occurred when new laws were enacted in the 1960's.

Chapter 5

The Roaring Twenties

The effort to control capitalism had begun years earlier and the attempt to control the consumption of alcohol was ratified on January 29, 1919 when Nebraska agreed to the Eighteenth Amendment of the Constitution. The amendment prohibited the production and sale of alcoholic beverages. The effort to control capitalism eventually became successful but the failure of the Eighteenth Amendment was caused by the strong resentment of it by a large segment of society. Most of the beer makers were Germans who had brought that skill with them when large numbers had immigrated earlier to America. Prohibition created an environment where the political and law enforcement officials began to solicit bribes to look the other way. Excessive corruption within government began to lead to excesses in the way the general population began to conduct themselves.

During this time, a rather obscure politician, Warren G. Harding (1865-1923), had been elected as a senator from Ohio. The only success he had had in his private life was when he owned the Marion Star. The newspaper was successful and well thought of throughout Ohio. He married a local banker's daughter, Florence Kling DeWolfe. She was a woman who dominated Hardinge and aspired to be the wife of a successful politician. With her encouragement, he entered politics where he had such early success he caught the attention of Harry M. Daugherty, an Ohio Republican king-maker. It was through his guidance that Harding became the U.S. Senator from Ohio.[1]

Theodore Roosevelt had planned for another try at the White House after Woodrow Wilson was re-elected in 1916. Hardinge had attempted to push a bill through the Senate which would have allowed former President Theodore Roosevelt to raise a volunteer army during World War I. It failed to pass and was looked upon as just one more sign of the incompetency of Hardinge. Roosevelt died in 1919 before he could put together the campaign for the presidency. He had considered Harding to be his vice-president running mate to pay him back for the attempt he made on Roosevelt's behalf to raise the volunteer army. Upon Roosevelt's death, the Republican party was in disarray. Harry Daugherty took advantage of the situation and in the legendary "smoke filled room" of the Convention, he was successful in having Harding named the nominee.[2]

Harding was inaugurated President on March 4, 1921 after having defeated Woodrow Wilson in a landslide during the 1920 election. He brought Daugherty with him to Washington to serve in his cabinet. It was Daugherty and a few other appointees who would lead the administration into a corrupt environment. Harding, though he was not notably corrupt, however, had a loyalty to his friends and would not allow himself to see the corruption among them. One little tidbit of corruption on behalf of Harding, though, was his hypocritical position pertaining to alcohol. Though he forbid the use of alcohol on the first floor of the White House, he served bootleg whiskey to his friends as they played poker on the second floor.

The corruptions within the Harding administration and the free wheeling society led to a national environment of excessiveness during the twenties. Speakeasies and bootlegging alcohol was a means to challenge the laws which the public deemed wrong. Many of the Americans found it exciting to flaunt the laws while seeking fun and entertainment. Al Capone and others like him became heroes to the people who lived in the world of "excitement".

A sudden heart attack felled Harding in August 1923. This occurred before the Teapot Dome and other scandals were uncovered. Two of his appointees went to prison as a result of their corruption. Unfortunately Warren G. Hardinge's administration is looked upon by history as very corrupt but at least he did not live to see the corruption surface. Perhaps the free wheeling society and the corruption within the Harding administration were reflective of times to come.

Calvin Coolidge (1872-1933) became President upon the death of Warren G. Harding in August 1923. His personal philosophy about government was that it should function as the enforcer of the laws by which the people should responsibly live. When Coolidge was a young man, Lord Salisbury had governed Britain. Salisbury made a statement concerning the role of government which Coolidge accepted as part of his philosophy of government. He had stated,

"The country is carried comfortably down the river by the current, and the function of government is merely to put out an oar when there is danger of its drifting into the bank."[3]

President Coolidge believed the better business conducted itself the less government would be required to act to assure adequate competition. If that were accomplished successfully, government could then concentrate on the economy and improve the national structure which would allow businessmen to perform their tasks. Those tasks, as Coolidge saw them, was for business to increase profits and investment, raise wages and provide better goods and services at the lowest possible prices.[4] That is also my personal view. However, the government should be cognizant of what business is doing. Observing, without dictating, the government should determine whether they are adhering to their responsibility of creating jobs for the people, paying fair wages, and providing better goods and services at the lowest possible prices. His standing aside and trusting the business community led to a dangerous economic situation. A false economic prosperity began to develop because of the free wheeling philosophy the American businessmen and people exhibited. The excesses, which became common after World War I, were left to the "law of economics". As I have stated before, the "law of economics" allows for economic cycles which fluctuate from much to little to much again.

Such excesses spilled into the investment world. People heard how others were making a lot of money in the stock market. They were not considering the money placed in the stock market as an investment. It was looked upon as "betting on the horses". Many times I have heard people who were in their twenties and thirties during the 1920s use that phrase when I mentioned to them in the 1960s that I was investing some money in stocks. Most of the money placed in the stock market prior to the twenties had come from upper middle class and above who considered themselves investors and were making their extra money work for them.

That viewpoint changed, though, when the average working man began to get involved with "making their fortunes by investing in America". With very little knowledge and very little money, the worker from the factory began "to play the ponies" so to speak. They began to rely upon the brokers to guide them to making their fortune. As in every aspect of life, there were unscrupulous individuals among those who were brokers. The brokerage industry was lightly regulated during the 1920s which allowed for many abuses. The Security Exchange was not established until 1934.

The unscrupulous individuals who were experienced in the workings of the stock market used this environment to manipulate the prices of stocks. They would conspire within a group to purchase stocks at low prices and then run up the prices of these stocks within their group. Sound familiar? Remember Jay Gould and the Erie Railroad Company? The small investors were persuaded to purchase the stocks which were being manipulated with the extra money they had as a result of higher wages. They trusted their brokers but did not have enough knowledge about the stock market to realize they were being used by the brokers to make large profits on the very same stocks they were being persuaded to buy.

The small investors were required to put up only ten percent when they purchased the stock. After having made a significant profit on the amount of money they had invested, their brokers persuaded them to "churn" their portfolios which continued the demand for stocks. As an example, they were required to put up $100 to purchase $1,000 of stock. When the value of their "gamble" went up twenty percent to $1,200, the small investor had doubled his $100, sold the stock and moved on to make more purchases. They now had enough capital to purchase $2,000 worth of stock. I realize I am not taking into account the commissions and other expenses but for simplicity purposes, this is a demonstration of how the small investor was doubling his capability to invest in more stock quickly. Up and away went the stock market with no top in sight.

With only a ten percent margin required, even the banks became involved. The small investors provided the ten percent margin necessary to purchase stocks while the banks loaned the remaining ninety percent with the stock used as collateral. As long as the stock prices were rising, there was no danger of margin calls. The increasing equity provided the collateral needed to protect the loans.

The American people began to feel rich because of the easy growth in the value of their stock assets. However, there was not enough money being spent on manufactured goods to prevent the manufacturing inventories from rising. Unemployment had been on the rise for a number of years and the demand for goods produced had been declining. In August of 1923, the United States Steel finally relented to pressure from the federal government and instituted the 8-hour day. This was a milestone for Labor. The workers had been accustomed to working 12 to 14 hours a day for every day of the week. U.S. Steel, which should have already been cutting production due to the business climate but had been reluctant to do so, benefitted by the reduction. Other industries followed U.S. Steel's lead. The economy was in decline.[5]

Not only was unemployment continuing to rise but those who were working were required to take wage reductions. As a result, the amount of money available to put into the stock market began to decline. In February of 1929, the Federal Reserve forbid the member banks from loaning money to anyone who was using it to purchase stocks.[6] This had the affect of drying up the "pyramid money" even further. Consequently, stock prices continued to decline precipitously. The small investor did not have any funds available to put up when the banks demanded more money to protect their collateral. As a result, the banks forced the sale of the stocks bought on ten-percent margins which brought even lower prices. The small investors lost 100% of their money which had been used to purchase the stocks on margin. With the swift decline in stock prices, even the banks lost huge sums of money. Some of the banks who had become involved in margin loans were forced to close due to insufficient funds. The stock market declined dramatically on October 24, 1929 despite efforts by J.P. Morgan and John D. Rockefeller to prop up the market. The final collapse occurred on October 29, 1929 which eventually led to what has become known as the Great Depression of the 1930s.[7]

Lack of adequate government regulations relating to where investors obtained funds to invest in the stock market had created a market which was nothing more than a "house of cards". This type of stock market had activated the economic law of supply and demand which had produced an unrealistically high stock market. With inadequate funds available to support the stock market it became a

51

market that was almost worthless on October 29, 1929. Had the investors been required to put greater than ten-percent into the purchase of stocks, the wild-fire speculations would have never gained a foothold. The possibility for an investor to double their money quickly had been monumental. Imagine how easy it was for those with a great deal of money to move in quickly with only the required ten-percent down and move out with ten's of thousands of dollars profits using the principle stated above. When the stock market declined dramatically, both the small and large investors lost a great deal of money which killed the "golden goose".

Chapter 6

A Changing Political Climate

The Bolshevik Party had overthrown the Czar of Russia in 1917 and formed a communist state. World War I was still being fought with Germany. The new government in Russia signed a peace treaty with Germany and withdrew from the war. On November 11, 1918, the war ended when Germany and the Allies of Western Europe and the United States signed a Peace Treaty. With the end of the war came much social unrest. The Communist Party in Russia became very active throughout Europe as they began to spread their doctrine of communism as an economic form of government.

In August of 1919, the Communist Party of America was founded in Chicago. Most of the first members were from Russia. By January of 1920, the nation had become caught in a war psychology without a war in sight. Attorney General A. Mitchell Palmer felt there was a "Red Menace" rising in America. Without bothering to obtain warrants, he authorized raids in private homes and labor headquarters. During one night in 33 separate cities, 4,000 people were seized and arrested for virtually no cause. Nothing was found which would have been judged as imminent revolutionary, but that did not bother Palmer. He was basking in the public adulation throughout the country which was an aftermath of the hysteria raised by him.[1]

The Republican Party controlled the White House throughout the 1920s with Warren G. Harding (1921-1923), Calvin Coolidge (1923-1928), and Herbert Hoover (1928-1932) being the occupants. Harding's time in the White House was tarnished by the uproar which became known as the Teapot Dome scandals. Coolidge presided over a period of exciting but troubled prosperity. Hoover was the unfortunate person to be in the White House when the stock market crashed in 1929 and the economy crumbled. Though he attempted to calm the fears and problems in America, he was ineffective in doing so. The future in America looked very gloomy. Unemployment had been rising since the early 1920s. Communism and socialism were gathering steam throughout the country.

America's business community had very little concern about the severity of the collapse which had taken place in the economy. Their attitude was to be against any government activity to combat the economic downturn for fear it would lead to greater regulations.[2] This played into Hoover's personal view. He felt the federal government's role was to do nothing. Entrepreneurs, who had created such a successful and prosperous economic cycle, were encouraged to work with state and local governments to bring about an end to the crisis. He continually told the American people that the economy had a solid base upon which a recovery could be developed. It goes almost without saying that his efforts of persuasion failed.

While Hoover was telling the American people that things would get better, Treasury Secretary Andrew Mellon, of the wealthy Mellon family, thought that the crisis was "not altogether a bad thing. People, he argued, will work harder, live a more moral life. Values will be adjusted, and enterprising people will pick up the wrecks from less competent people."[2]

One theory which Hoover advanced was to provide some aid to the large corporations with the view that the money would "trickle down" to the people. In this case, it never did. America will repeat this theory in the future during the Reagan presidency. More on the results of that experiment will be presented later.

Many people in America felt capitalism had failed them. They were unemployed with no hope of employment. This made them susceptible to the message the communists and socialists proclaimed. The Communist Party of America spoke of a good life in the Soviet Union where everyone was employed and shared equally in the rewards of their labor. They insisted that now was the time for the workers in America to get their fair share of the wealth. In Russia, Joseph Stalin had been in power since the mid-1920s following the death of Lenin. He had begun the first Five Year Plan in 1928 which established goals for the Russian economy every five years. The first plan had not been as successful as the communists in America implied but they didn't mention that in their effort to gain the trust of the workers.[3]

During the 1920s, the workers had not listened to the claims of the Communist Party because of the prosperous economy. Now, in the 1930s, there was beginning to be some doubt about capitalism in the minds of the unemployed. Riots and marches broke out throughout America. A feeling of revolt began to develop, suggesting whether capitalism would survive as the American economic system. Could communism serve the workers better?

When Hoover's "trickle down" effort to ease the hardships of the Depression failed to solve the economic problems, the American people lost faith in him. The Democrats realized they had an opportunity in 1932 to capture the office of President and gain control of Congress. At their convention in Chicago, they nominated Franklin D. Roosevelt, who had been the vice-president candidate in 1928. President Hoover was nominated again by the Republican Party to carry their banner in 1932. He spent most of his time during the campaign defending his administration's policies and efforts to bring an end to the Depression. Roosevelt, on the other hand, conducted a campaign where he offered a new deal for the American people but he did not go into much detail about it. The electorate showed their distrust of Hoover by electing Roosevelt who carried all but six states.[4]

Roosevelt took office in March of 1933 after the election of November 1932. During the time between the election and his inauguration, the economy reached the lowest level of the Depression. Many banks were failing. It became so troublesome in Detroit that the governor ordered all the banks throughout the state to close for eight days. This began to cause panics throughout the rest of the nation. Depositors began withdrawing large amounts of money before their banks would be closed. The banks did not have enough liquid assets to cover these withdrawals. Consequently, the governors of forty states were forced to order the banks within their jurisdiction to be closed. To make matters worse, the New York Stock Exchange shut down.[4]

Shortly after his inauguration, Roosevelt declared a national "bank holiday". The American people strongly disapproved the closing of the banks. Though Congress wanted to nationalize the banking system, Roosevelt proposed a bill which would empower the government to lend money to troubled banks. Further, the bill would allow the reorganization of failed banks and the hoarding of gold was to be stopped. The government soon permitted those banks which were solvent to reopen. It was not long before the public began to make more deposits into the banks than was being withdrawn.[5]

The Democrats had won an overwhelming majority in both the Senate and House of Representatives during the 1932 elections. With the support of a heavily Democrat congress, Roosevelt was now in the position to put forth a program which the American people hoped would alleviate their problems. He used the radio to make speeches of encouragement, the first of which was his inaugural speech. In that speech, he said to America his now famous quote "the only thing we have to fear is fear itself". Roosevelt believed in capitalism as an economic system. He desired to bring back the economy with programs which would give hope to the people through job creations by both public and business efforts. Although he was accused of promoting communism by the business community and the Republicans, such activity was far from his belief.

During the first hundred days of his administration, Congress passed legislation to provide immediate relief, promote economic recovery, and strengthen government regulation of the economy. The Senate passed a bill, which had been backed by the AFL, that would have created a thirty-hour work week for all factories where the goods they produced were for interstate sale. The supporters claimed more jobs would be created by the bill and labor would receive a larger share of wealth being created by their work efforts. Roosevelt did not support the bill; instead he proposed a bill which would establish the National Industrial Recovery Act.[6]

The NIRA permitted the businesses to regulate themselves. It also stipulated that the government would be responsible for providing jobs for the unemployed. One section of the bill set up a major public works program which was used to promote employment by the construction of bridges, roads, dams and other projects. These projects were to be administered by the Public Works Administration. An important part of the Act was Section 7a. The employees of companies were given the right to organize as unions and bargain with the management through their elected representatives. No longer could the employers restrain or coerce the workers in these activities. Employers were not permitted to require employees to join company unions and sign "yellow-dog" contracts as a stipulation of employment. Individual industry codes or the President of the United States could set maximum working hours and minimum wages.[7] This meant the employers of America could operate their companies in a capitalistic manner but were required to follow certain rules which were established by the government to prevent the past practices of unscrupulous employers.

During the early part of the 1920s and continuing into the Depression, union membership had fallen dramatically. Unions had been considered unnecessary by the workers during the "boom" of the twenties. Now the workers did not want to "rock the boat" in the early stages of the Depression. As long as they had a job they had no desire to confront employers about wages and working conditions. That attitude changed, however, with the passage of the NIRA. Employees felt more secure with the federal government protecting their rights to collective bargaining. The effects of the Depression and Roosevelt's election had created an uncertainty throughout industry about government support pertaining to labor relations. As a result, the unions made the decision to become more aggressive in their effort to increase union membership.

One of the first unions to make a strong move to increase their membership was the United Mine Workers of America which was under the leadership of John L. Lewis. Lewis, at times, was looked upon as a radical but that was not true. During the 1920s, he had been a Republican and was a bitter opponent of left-wing unionism. His goal was to organize the labor movement by industry, not by craft. Using patriotism and Roosevelt's popularity, organizers in Kentucky put on an all out campaign to sign up new members in the coal mines. Circulars were passed throughout Kentucky which stated that the NIRA recommended the miners form their own union. One even went so far as to suggest that the President wanted the workers to join the union.[8]

With an increasing membership and his close relationship with President Roosevelt in hand, Lewis pressured the coal operators to accept the union's proposals for the NRA code which covered the bituminous coal industry. Following a series of wildcat strikes, in September 1933 the operators conceded to the union's demands. The concessions were higher wages, reduced variations in pay throughout different areas in the country, the use of child labor was prevented, and the establishment of an eight-hour work day and the five-day work week. Further concessions were made which permitted miners to select their own check-weighman, and one of the most important concessions was forbidding the use of scrip for wage payments. The balance of power in the coal industry was now seen as belonging to the union. With that reversal came the achievement of many of its longstanding goals.[9]

There was much physical strife in the labor and employer relationship throughout the nation. In Toledo, Ohio, which was a major center for the manufacturing of automobile parts, workers in several of the plants organized an AFL local. In February of 1934, 4,000 auto workers went on a strike which lasted six days. A modest increase in wages and an agreement to negotiate other issues were accomplished by the strike. Electric Auto-Lite, one of the large companies, refused to negotiate at which time the walkout began again. The management decided to hire scabs to keep their plants operating.[10]

The American Workers Party, which was a local unemployed organization of socialists, joined the struggling strikers. Together they formed large picket lines which were in defiance of a court injunction. The local law enforcement officials, and special deputies who were paid by Auto-Lite management, arrested some of the picket leaders and also beat an old man. This caused "all hell to break loose" and what has been called the Battle of Toledo began. The Auto-Lite plant was blocked by a crowd of 10,000 for seven hours. The intention of the blockade was to prevent the strikebreakers who were inside from leaving. In an effort to disperse the crowd, special deputies used tear gas, water hoses and occasional gunfire but the crowds reacted by throwing stones toward the plants and burning cars in the parking lot. Following this day of violence, the National Guard was called in the next day when violence broke out again. This time two protesters were killed by the Guard. When that failed to stop the strike, the Commander of the National Guard ordered the plant to be closed. Two weeks of federal mediation finally resulted in an agreement which called for recognition of the union, a higher minimum wage, and a five percent raise in wages.[10]

Behind much of the labor strife could be found the Socialist and Communist Parties. Harry Bridges, an Australian-born longshoreman, worked closely with the Communist Party and signed up many new members to form a local union of the International Longshoremen's Association (ILA). It was a struggle for the new local as they not only had to fight the local employers but, also, the conservative national leaders of the East Coast ILA.[11]

The West Coast longshoremen threatened to strike in the spring of 1934 but the threat was canceled at the request of President Roosevelt. A secret agreement was reached with the employers by the ILA leaders but the agreement was rejected by the rank and file workers. They felt the agreement fell short of their demands for a shorter workweek and higher pay. Union recognition, and union-run hiring halls were demanded. The halls were to replace "shape-ups" which was the present way of hiring individual dock workers. The longshoremen in San Francisco defied the national ILA leaders and went on strike May 9. Soon the dockworkers in every West Coast ports, with the exception of Los Angeles, joined in the strike. When sailors and waterfront truckers also stopped working, 40,000 maritime workers from Seattle to San Diego were on strike. This was the largest such strike by the maritime industry that had been ever seen. Two months later, the employers knew the strike would not end on its own. Taking action on July 3, they used the police and newly hired scabs to attempt to get the maritime industry functioning again. As one would expect, violence broke out and two strikers were shot and killed by the police and scores of strikers were seriously hurt.[11]

When word spread about the event on the docks, workers throughout San Francisco were outraged and called for a general strike. Union leaders were afraid they were about to lose control of their unions so they reluctantly went along with the strike. By July 16, San Francisco was practically at a stand still as 130,000 workers throughout the city walked off their jobs. This general strike was short lived, however. Local businessmen, newspapers, and government officials attempted to split the ranks of labor.

Longshoremen's leaders were denounced as dangerous radicals while vigilante groups were encouraged to destroy the offices of the Communist Party and several allied organizations. The NRA's Hugh Johnson joined in the rhetoric by calling the strike a "bloody insurrection". Under this kind of pressure, the General Strike Committee slowly allowed more workers to return to work. On July 19, the Committee called off the general strike. The striking waterfront unions were forced to accept arbitration. However, out of that arbitration came recognition for the union, hiring halls that the union could effectively control, a thirty-hour workweek, and a pay increase.[12]

In the strikes which took place in Toledo and San Francisco, the Socialists and Communists, while defying the conservative AFL leaders, were able to activate thousands of working people into an army of militant participants. This established them as a force to be reckoned with in the future. America was still not out of the woods as far as the influence of these two groups was concerned. Labor was beginning to become disillusioned with the efforts of the Roosevelt administration to overcome the affects of the Great Depression. National income had risen by one-quarter but was still approximately half of what it had been in 1929. Even though unemployment had dropped by two million and factory wages had risen, there were still ten million workers without jobs. The most distressing statistic was that almost twice the number of unemployed were at least partially dependent on relief. Secretary of Treasury Henry Morgenthau, Jr. stated that "we are not making any headway".[13]

The first two years of Roosevelt's term in the White House did not bring about the positive changes that had been expected. In spite of the self confidence he displayed, FDR's New Deal plan had not ended the distress which was prevalent throughout America. A more pro-active plan would have to be developed. Somehow the government and businesses had to be brought together. Such a task would be difficult because of the distrust the businessmen had of Roosevelt. The future of capitalism in America was still being challenged during those first two years.

During the 1935 Chamber of Commerce annual meeting, Silas Strawn described the anger many businessmen felt concerning FDR and the New Deal by stating "We have floundered along for two years without knowing whether we are going to be locked up or not...businessmen are tired of hearing promises to do constructive things, which turn out to be only attempts to Sovietize America."[14]

Chapter 7

Roosevelt's Next Two Years

The Supreme Court ruled the National Industrial Recovery Act codes unconstitutional in May 1935. A bill named the National Labor Relations had been introduced in February 1935 by Robert E. Wagner, the senator from New York At first Roosevelt had opposed it while seeking compliance of the NIRA by the business community. When the NIRA was declared unconstitutional, he decided to support Wagner's bill. In June, the Wagner Act was passed by Congress and signed by Roosevelt. The bill gave workers the right to choose their own union to represent them to management. Other rights given the workers were the right to strike, the right to boycott, and the right to picket. Employers could no longer conduct what was considered unfair labor acts such as financing of company unions, arbitrary dismissal of activists, refusing to bargain with a union, blacklisting of employees and hiring industrial spies. A new National Labor Relations Board had been named. If workers requested the right to select who would represent them, the NLRB would conduct the election. Once more the employers had to comply with "a rule of conduct" within the capitalistic system.[1]

The Democrats began to form a new national political coalition which embraced workers and their labor organizations. John L. Lewis had pointed out to the American Federation of Labor (AFL) that large numbers of corporations had joined together for the purpose of having enough power to oppose the AFL. They had already shown they were 100% effective in doing so. He presented an analogy that if the AFL would attempt to unionize large corporations with a craft union concept, they would be slaughtered in the same manner that Italian machine guns will cut down the Ethiopians in the war occurring in that country.[2]

Lewis contacted several separate union leaders. His idea was to consider a separate organization from the AFL. The purpose of the new organization was to gather the workers of the mass production and unorganized industries in America. The new organization was named the Committee for Industrial Organization. This did not set well with the leaders of the AFL who immediately demanded the new organization be dissolved. When John L. Lewis and the other labor leaders in the new organization refused to do so, the AFL suspended and later expelled all the unions involved in the new organization.

The CIO, which changed it's name to Congress of Industrial Organizations, went onto the labor scene as an underdog compared to the AFL. When John L. Lewis and the CIO became very prominent in the re-election campaign of FDR in 1936, they gained a great deal of national prestige. The AFL supported Roosevelt, also, but in a more reserved way. Even the Socialist and Communist Parties, who had candidates on the ballot, gave their support to Roosevelt by running campaigns where they implicitly backed him. The Socialist candidate, Norman Thomas, commented that socialism is the system which will save us but short of that it is better to follow the Roosevelt administration. When asked in the future about his campaign in 1936, Communist Party chairman Earl Browder said his campaign had been an ambiguous one in favor of Roosevelt.[3]

Roosevelt ran a campaign which emphasized the accomplishments of his previous two years when he had begun what became known as The Second New Deal. The Republicans nominated Kansas governor, Alfred Lanford who ran a campaign criticizing Roosevelt for increasing the federal deficit and undermining the Constitution, the dollar and the free market. His campaign did not resonate with the American people and FDR received 60 percent of the popular votes and lost only Vermont and Maine in the electoral votes. So overwhelming was the election that the Democrats picked up twelve more seats in the House of Representatives which gave them 75 percent of the total seats. Seven new Democrat senators gave them almost 80 percent control in the Senate. The attempt to control capitalism in America was now solidified. What the long term effect would be was still to be determined.[3]

The labor movement picked up steam. Most of the increase in union activity was in the auto industry. Time after time the auto plants encountered angry workers who would not allow the companies to speed-up the production lines. They felt the foremen were disrespectful towards them and were determined to not allow such treatment. This marked the beginning of a militant era for the auto workers. Labor leaders, corporate executives, the police or politicians were unable to control the actions of the workers. The United Auto Workers (UAW), a new union which had begun as an affiliate of the AFL in 1935, became dissatisfied with the effort by AFL president Green to select the UAW leadership and dictate its organizing strategy. They bolted from the AFL to join the CIO in the summer of 1936.[4]

To better the pay and working conditions of the auto workers, the UAW decided to take on the largest company, General Motors. While the union leaders were developing a plan to take on General Motors, the workers took action of their own. They began to stage a sit down at their work stations and refused to work. This was done to protest wage cuts which GM had put into effect. In the Cleveland Fisher Body plant, workers in one department sat down in protest and the other 7,000 employees joined them. When the managers in Flint's Fischer Body Plant No. 2 attempted to discipline three union members, fifty workers occupied the building. The event angered the workers from the Fisher No. 1 plant. They demanded their leaders allow them to shut down the No. 1 plant. The workers returned to the No. 1 plant where between 500 to 1,000 workers gained control of the factory and within minutes the assembly line was shut down. The occupation of the buildings prevented GM managers from hiring scabs to continue production. It also prevented them from asking the police to remove the striking workers because the plant property and expensive equipment could be damaged. A Gallup poll showed that a majority of Americans believed the strikers should leave the plant but GM should not use force to evict them.[5]

After failing to get a court injunction, the GM executives decided to take action to end the stalemate. The heat was turned off by the guards upon orders from the executives. Orders were also given to the guards to prevent strike sympathizers on the outside from bringing food to the workers occupying the plant. They were unable to do so when the workers inside the plant forced the gates open which allowed the sympathizers to deliver the food. At this point, GM called in the police who stormed the plant. When the police gained entrance to the plant, they were confronted by the workers who turned fire hoses on them and also dropped two-pound car hinges upon their heads. The police withdrew and developed plans for a second attempt which was also repelled. The police began to open fire with their guns wounding several workers. A third attempt to break the sit-down strike failed, and the police withdrew from the plant grounds and would not return again. Because of this strong stand by the sit-down strikers, other GM workers who had previously declined to join the union lined up at the UAW headquarters to sign membership cards and pay their dues.[6]

The workers inside the plant decided they had to confront the situation they were in by establishing some semblance of order. A committee was formed which represented every department within the plant. They established rules concerning the conduct of each worker involved in the sit-down. If a worker broke one of the rules, he had to appear before a committee where it was explained why his conduct could not be tolerated. They did not want it to appear they had trashed the plant while the sit-down tactic took place. Plans were developed whereby meals were obtained from outside, sanitation needs were met, defensive actions, if required, were established and entertainment to while away the time was provided.[7]

When the Governor of Michigan, Frank Murphy ordered 1500 National Guard members to Flint, he tried to persuade the workers to leave. He promised negotiations as a means to end the stalemate but General Motors nullified that suggestion. The workers remained in defiance of GM, the Flint police, and Governor Murphy and refused to leave. GM wanted Murphy to send the Guard into the plants to break the siege but the Governor refused to do so. Roosevelt learned of the situation and wanted a negotiated end to the strike. He opposed using troops to end the stalemate but he did feel that the workers tactics were wrong.[8]

The UAW developed a plan which eventually caused GM to give up the struggle to prevent the unionization of their plants. The leaders felt they could win the strike if they shut down Flint's Chevrolet plant No. 4. This plant was the only source for engines that were used in every Chevrolet automobile. Knowing they could not rush past the General Motors plant guards, they decided to use the GM spies who had infiltrated their ranks during the strike. They circulated their plan to rush Chevrolet Plant No. 9 in an effort to shut down that operation. The spies informed the General Motors management that Plant 9 would soon be the target of a takeover by the strikers. Guards of other plants, including Plant 4, were moved to Plant 9 to prevent such action. With Plant 4 virtually unguarded, the workers went to Plant 4 where they entered unopposed. There were approximately 4,000 workers inside Plant 4, one half of which joined in the sit-down movement while the other half left the plant. This move halted the production of the motors needed for the production of Chevrolets. General Motors succumbed to the union's demand to negotiate their grievances.[9]

The company conceded to the UAW their right of recognition as the representative of the workers at all the plants which were on strike. They also agreed to not create company unions for six months. Other concessions were to drop all lawsuits related to the strike and to not discipline any of the strikers. GM agreed that all other demands of the UAW would be discussed at a national labor-management conference. The workers could now speak openly about their union activities. Having shown that there was strength in unity, the workers began to rely on militant, on-the-spot collective action to gain further concessions. The battle to obtain concessions from the company had just begun and would continue for several years. It was the beginning of the union's power which would lead to abuse in the future.[9]

The defeat of General Motors had long reaching consequences for not only the automobile industry but also many of the large manufacturing companies in America. U.S. Steel president Myron Taylor decided all of industry would eventually have to deal with the unions in the way General Motors had done so. To prevent violent occurrences in his company, he contacted John L. Lewis of the CIO and Philip Murray of the Steel Workers' Organizing Committee and consented to recognize the CIO's (SWOC) as sole bargaining agent for U.S. Steel's workers. He also granted a 10 percent pay raise, reduced the standard work-week to forty hours with time and a half pay for work over the standard work-week.[10]

Approximately 4.7 million workers were involved in some kind of strike action during 1937, which was nearly twice as many as the previous year. Through the organizing efforts of the unions, the membership of the CIO had grown to above 3.7 million by September 1937. The AFL was also benefitting by the growth in union membership. They began organizing workers which they had previously ignored. In many small and decentralized industries, AFL unions successfully competed against the CIO for new members. In fact, many anti-union employers who were frightened by the CIO successes were now willing to negotiate with AFL unions to avoid having to deal with "Lewis's Reds."[11]

With the storm clouds of war forming in Europe, Roosevelt began to focus his attention on world events and less on domestic affairs. Even though the statistics which came out in 1938 indicated that the Depression was worsening, he felt the world events had to be monitored more closely. Former President Hoover made a speech in 1938 where he openly disagreed with Roosevelt about creating alliances with those European countries who were lining up against the Fascist states such as Germany, Italy and Spain. Hoover warned that such alliances would only lead to war.[12]

Roosevelt's response was to submit a budget in January of 1939 of $9 billion which included $1.3 billion for defense.[13] Later, in January of 1940, the budget he submitted to Congress had a request of $1.8 billion for defense out of a total $8.4 billion budget.[14] This represented a 21 percent defense request in 1940 compared to 14.4 percent in 1939. The control of capitalism was placed on the low heat back burner as the possibility of war became more likely. The government knew they would need the industrial might in America to fight any war which may occur.

Japan was beginning to cause grave concerns in Washington with its militant activities in Asia. In September 1940, Roosevelt announced an embargo which would take effect in October on the export of scrap steel and iron outside of the Western Hemisphere. The only exception was Great Britain. Japan officially protested the embargo to the U.S. Government on October 8, 1940. They needed the supply of scrap steel and iron to continue their activities.

In anticipation of a future war, Roosevelt presented a budget of $17.4 billion to Congress in January 1941. A defense budget of $10.8 billion reflected his concern. The defense portion of the budget had risen from 21 percent of total budget in 1940 to 62 percent of total budget in 1941. With such increases in government spending, the grip of the Great Depression was beginning to be broken.[15]

In keeping with the intent of this book, events pertaining to the attack of Pearl Harbor by the Japanese on December 7, 1941 and the subsequent declaration of war against Germany, Italy and Japan will not become part of my presentation. Labor continued to advance their cause in the period just before World War II. In January 1941, Roosevelt declared that "Whatever stands in the way of speed and efficiency in defense preparations must give way to the national needs." He added, "We should not stop work for a single day. If any dispute arises we shall keep on working until the dispute is solved by mediation, conciliation, or arbitration—until the war is won."[16]

Sidney Hillman was appointed by Roosevelt to an important defense mobilization post. Defense contractors, conservative members of congress, and military leaders joined the White House in demanding an end to ongoing industrial disputes which were considered a drain on defense production by the War Department. CIO unions which were on strike at several defense sites assented to call off their strikes at Hillman's suggestion. The AFL, likewise, agreed to end their strikes at any location considered a defense related location. Roosevelt had set up a National Defense Mediation Board in early 1941. Many of the labor/management disputes were prevented from becoming a negative factor in the production of defense material. Incidents of government imposed wage increases, however, were the reason for ending many of the work-stoppages.[16]

Chapter 8

Federal Government's Role Begins to Change

President Franklin D. Roosevelt was re-elected in 1940 when he defeated Wendell Willkie by collecting 449 electoral college votes to Willkie's 82. Americans indicated they still favored Roosevelt's programs. With World War II being conducted against the Axis Powers since 1941, defense expenditures had created a "boom" economy. Full employment (including women and African-American factory workers) meant the American people were patriotically behind President Roosevelt.

When the 1944 election was held, Roosevelt easily won re-election by defeating Thomas E. Dewey (432 electoral votes to 99). Little did the nation realize that former Senator Harry S. Truman, the vice-president candidate Roosevelt had selected, would soon become President Harry S. Truman. He was a man of whom the public knew very little. When Roosevelt died in Warm Spring, Georgia on April 12, 1945, the nation was stunned and pondered what would happen in America without the leadership of Roosevelt.[1]

Truman's background was somewhat controversial because of the political connection with the T.J. Pendegrast political machine in earlier years. Despite much corruption by many of the people surrounding him during the time he was judge of the Jackson County Court in Missouri, he was never found to be involved in any corrupt practices throughout his life. He was considered by many who knew him to be a poor businessman but he was an outstanding administrator. It was his family and school which provided him with a firm background in religious and moral standards which he carried as his banner. He felt strongly about personal and national responsibility. These strengths, which he carried into the office of President when Roosevelt died, enabled him to become a better national and world leader than anyone thought he was capable of becoming.

Following World War II, the role of the federal government began to change. In 1946, while the Democrats still controlled congress, the

Employment Act of 1946 was passed. It was this Act which gave the federal government the responsibility and power to promote maximum employment, production, and purchasing power. It also set up a Council of Economics Advisers which was given the responsibility to develop economic policies for the nation. Government was to now become involved in the economic stability of America with an attempt to control the "laws of economics". They began by developing a government policy which was based on the theories developed by British economist John Maynard Keynes. His theory was that capitalist economic systems could be regulated to prevent the booms and busts of the past. He advocated the governments use their taxing and spending power to control the demand for goods and services throughout the nation.[2] The controlling of capitalism was now to become a partnership between government, labor and capitalists.

Walter Reuther of the UAW, who was a former socialist, determined that higher income and stable prices was the direction he felt the nation should take. He wanted to see a 30 percent wage increase for autoworkers. In his opinion, that would equal the income which was lost when the number of hours constituting a work week was reduced from sixty to forty. He further suggested that the automobile companies management should hold the price of cars at prewar levels.[3]

Thus began the era of labor's pressure for wage increases without considering the factors of business costs and prices. When labor went on strike, their demands were for higher wages or shorter work weeks without any reduction in wages. Several different unions went on strike during the early part of 1946. These strikes caused some disruptions in the lives of the public. With the majority of the workforce in America not unionized, these strikes began to change the public's view of the unions. However, due to pressure from the government to not create problems for the economy of the country, the businessmen granted such union requests even though they knew prices would have to be increased at a later date.

To prevent a worsening inflation, Truman's proposal to the nation was to continue the rationing. He further proposed a plan to raise the minimum wage and increase the unemployment compensation along with putting it under the control of the federal government. Another of his proposals was to appropriate billions of dollars which would be used for a nationwide housing program. Labor's view that industry could afford to give an inflation free wage increase to the workers was supported by Secretary of Commerce Henry Wallace and Office of Price Administration chief Chester Bowles.[4] That view reflected a lack of understanding the rationale of their proposals. In order for a company to continue in business, they must make a profit to enable them to create jobs and, also within our tax system, to provide tax revenue for the government. No company is "entitled" to profits, though. They must earn them. However, with such views of political and labor leaders, the task of earning a profit became more difficult.

The union leaders failed to realize that the American public does not like to stray too far from the middle ground of politics. A war had been fought and won and now the public wanted to get on with their lives without further disruptions. The people who had worked in the factories during the war had saved a tremendous amount of their earnings due to the lack of goods on which they could spend their money. With products now available, the public began to spend some of their savings on automobiles and other consumer goods.

Price controls remained, however, and were extended for another year in July of 1946. Home ownership was now high on the list of desires to be fulfilled by the returning veterans of World War II. The housing industry boomed and communities were built specifically to satisfy this demand. As in any economic system, when the demand exceeded the supply, a rapid growth of inflation swept the country. It was the only time I have known where a person could buy a new automobile and sell it later for a higher price than what they paid for it. This continued to be true for a period of time until the supply of new products caught up with the demand.

With the troubling inflation and the interruption in production of consumer goods caused by the many crippling strikes in the early part of 1946, the Republicans were able to persuade the American voters that they were more capable of handling the current problems than the Democrats. Consequently, in the 1946 elections, the Republicans gained control of the House of Representatives and the Senate for the first time since Roosevelt had swept the Democrats into congressional power in 1932. With the new makeup of congress, Truman now had to deal with a congressional leadership which wanted to weaken the power the unions had gained. They were also intent upon protecting the rights of the business community as they saw them. The Republicans not only had a majority in each chamber of Congress, but by joining with southern Democrats who shared similar views, they now had the power to override any vetoed legislation.

With a dissatisfied public behind them, the Republicans were successful in developing the Taft-Hartley Act in 1947. This legislation was guided through the House by New Jersey congressman Fred Hartley and Senator Robert Taft of Ohio guided it through the Senate. Truman vetoed the Bill when it reached his desk but Congress was able to override the veto. The Act made sympathy strikes and boycotts more difficult, and allowed states to ban the union shop. Since there was a drive on to unionize plants in the South, this was helpful for the states in the South and also the West. In order for the unions to participate in NLRB elections, their leaders had to state they were non-Communist. The leaders of big unions also knew they would be negotiating with companies knowing the President of the United States could prevent a strike by the union for eighty days by declaring a "national emergency". They felt this put them at a disadvantage.[5]

None of the above mentioned restrictions turned the law into the "slave labor law" which critics of the Taft-Hartley Law had suggested. The corporate leaders used the law to deradicalize the union movement. Their strategy was to confine the labor movement to its present area of influence. The law denoted a momentous change in the climate of class relations throughout the United States. In order to survive, the unions changed their goals of making more gains to just protecting the gains they had made in previous years. The concerns about social programs would have to take a back seat under the present political conditions.[6]

Such activities increased the perception in the eyes of the public that the union workers were selfish and untrustworthy. The unions began to lose their power in the struggle to influence the debate of workers job protection and work conditions. Non-union workers were enjoying equal or better conditions in their work environment.

Many of those conditions came as the result of the unions obtaining them first but owners of non-union factories granted them to their own employees if they could see the benefit in their own labor relations.

Such an example was the cost-of-living (COLA) in the wage agreement in 1948 which the UAW had won in the automotive industry. It was looked upon as an easy way for management to determine how much to increase their worker's pay each year by following a government produced statistic which showed the increase in the cost of living since the last pay raise. It was only later that such an approach was determined to be a negative factor in providing a stable economy. Such a benefit was responsible for "feeding inflation" by increasing wages automatically based on the rate of inflation without taking into consideration what effect the higher production costs would have on prices.

The reign of power which had begun in 1946 for the Republicans was short lived. The Republicans again nominated New York Governor Thomas E. Dewey for President in June of 1948. It was felt he would become the next President as Truman appeared to have lost his base voters. After he was re-nominated on the Democratic ticket in July, some of the Democrats bolted from the Party and formed a States Rights Party (Dixiecrats). Their presidential candidate was Strom Thurmond of South Carolina. The Progressive Party nominated Henry Wallace who had resigned from Truman's Administration in 1946 because of strong differences over the policies toward the Soviet Union. Wallace felt that America should have a closer relationship with the Soviet Union and had spoken out against Truman's policy towards them. At times his position was interpreted by his dissenters as his being a Communist.

An interesting sidelight concerning Wallace is that he was Roosevelt's Vice-President during the term before which Truman had been selected as Roosevelt's VP. It would be interesting to know what kind of country America would be today had Roosevelt died six months before the convention in 1944 or he had decided to retain Wallace as his VP candidate for another term.

Returning to the election of 1948, Truman defeated Dewey by 2.2 million popular votes and 114 electoral votes. His 10,000 mile "whistle stop" strategy late in the campaign showed Truman's ability to connect with the man on the street, in the factory, and on the farm. Control of congress was also returned to the Democrats.

Under the Truman Administration, government began to become a "Big Brother" to the American people. In July of 1949, Truman signed the Housing Act which provided for extended federal aid for public housing throughout the United States, which many hoped would alleviate the housing shortage in America. People began to look to Washington for help in their lives. In the triangle of labor, business, and government, labor and business were being pushed aside. Government's intrusion into the lives of the American people was gaining momentum.

One such intrusion took place on April 8, 1952 when President Truman signed Executive Order No. 10340 which authorized the seizure of the steel mills. A lengthy dispute between the union and management had poised a problem of insufficient steel to wage battle against the North Korean government. Truman said he was seizing the mills on a temporary basis for the purpose of national security. This action taken was caused by Truman's personal distrust of corporate leaders which had been his views for most of his life. Later, a Supreme Court which was composed of FDR and HST Justice appointees ruled that Truman did not have the authority to take such action.[7] This was a statement from the Judicial branch of government that capitalists were protected by the Constitution just as the common person on the street was protected.

It is strange that this movement towards government intrusion took place under Harry S. Truman. He had long been an advocate of personal responsibility. In fact, that was one of the basic strengths of his character. As an admirer of Truman, I have long wondered why he was willing to encourage the individual to begin relying on the government for their personal needs.

President Truman stated in March 1952 that he would not be a candidate for President in the upcoming federal elections. This left the Democrats with the first really open convention since 1932. They nominated Adlai Stevenson to run against Dwight D. Eisenhower who selected Senator Richard Nixon from California as his vice-president candidate. Stevenson selected Senator John Sparkman of Alabama as his running mate. Eisenhower easily defeated Stevenson in the November election by receiving 442 electoral votes to Stevenson's 89.[8]

During the Eisenhower Administration, the federal government began to look into the alleged infiltration of unions by organized crime. The purpose of such investigations was to ensure that the motives of the unions were for the good of their members. Movies, such as On the Waterfront, depicted the power which the union leaders used in a corrupt manner for their individual wealth. The AFL-CIO, which had combined in 1955, expelled David Beck from its Executive Committee. He was charged with "gross misuse of union funds". Subsequently, Beck was charged with tax evasion by a Federal grand jury in August of 1957. Further actions by the AFL-CIO to fight corruption resulted in the Teamsters' Union being expelled in December 1957.

President Eisenhower urged congress to pass legislation to prevent illegal labor union practices. His request was an attempt by the government to cut down on racketeering and other abuses in unions. The result of Eisenhower's request was the passage of the Landrum-Griffin Act in September of 1959. The Act provided the power of law which the government could use to help curb racketeering and blackmail in labor organizations.[9] Unions were no longer looked upon as respectable organizations by the general public. Fewer workers were interested in forming unions within their workplace.

Beginning in the 1950's, the American people began to use the government for the purpose of obtaining civil rights for African-Americans and others who had not shared in the prosperity which most of the population had attained. As previously mentioned, the unions, with the exception of the United Mine Workers, had marched forward without including the black workers in the effort to control capitalism in the workplace. After having fought in World War II for the freedoms to be found in America, the African-American began to demand equal opportunities in the workplace and educational facilities. The passage of the Civil Rights Act of 1964 prohibited discrimination towards anyone because of their race, color or creed. With the passage of the Civil Rights Act, the opportunity for a greater share of the economic pie in America became available to those who had been denied opportunities in the past.

In time, the large corporations began a more balanced approach in their hiring of workers and selected more African-Americans as foremen and managers. Large numbers of blacks were now enrolling at colleges and universities. Much could be written about the era during the civil rights movement. However, my thesis is concerning the control of capitalism. All Americans were now involved in controlling capitalism without fear of reprisal for their actions.

Chapter 9

Unrest in America

The War in Vietnam, the assassinations of President John F. Kennedy, Senator Robert Kennedy, and Dr. Martin Luther King led to much public unrest during the 1960s and 1970s. Anti-war views of the young draft age youths and college students led to many demonstrations. Some of the demonstrations which were held turned violent. Two tragic events became the focal point of the demonstrations. When Dr. King, who was the leader of the Civil Rights movement, was assassinated on April 4, 1968, riots occurred throughout the country. These riots had more to do with the assassination rather than social problems or economic problems. However, both of the problems were just beneath the surface of the riots.

A second event, which occurred on the campus of Kent State University in Ohio, was the killing of four students by the Ohio National Guard on May 4, 1970 during an anti-war demonstration.[1] This led to a hardening of the anti-war position of the youth in America. On May 8, anti-war demonstrators gathered outside a federal building on Wall Street in New York City. They had lowered the American flag to half staff in homage to the four students killed on May 4. About 200 construction workers with their hard hats on rushed the demonstrators and gained control of the flagpole and raised the flag back to full mast.[2]

My interpretation, at the time the May 8 event happened, was that the workers of America were getting angry at the demonstrators. Young people who espoused communism, socialism and anarchism had taken over the student movement. The workers were satisfied with what life in America had given them. They felt the demonstrators were threatening to bring down the government and economic system which provided them with the standard of living they were enjoying. Capitalism was being challenged in America and the workers, though they belonged to unions, were set to show the demonstrators they would take no more of the anti-capitalism activities.

A great deal of anger had been building against the demonstrators since the 1968 Democratic National Convention. The demonstrators outside the Convention Hall were intent on creating a disturbance which would disrupt the nomination of Hubert Humphrey as the Democrat's presidential candidate. Many of the demonstrators were arrested, including a group which were given the label of the "Chicago Seven". They were brought to trial, convicted and imprisoned.

Richard Nixon was elected President in November 1968, receiving a majority of the electoral votes. However, with three candidates running for President, Nixon had received less than 50% of the popular votes. This gave those who opposed him the opportunity to continuously refer to him as a "minority president". That label disturbed him greatly. He appeared to be a man who was overly concerned about what people thought of him.

Johnson had attempted to have a "butter and guns" economic policy during the Vietnam War. He felt the economy could handle supplying both the war effort and the substantial demand for consumer goods. This created rampant inflation which was left for Nixon to handle. One attempt by Nixon to control inflation was to freeze prices and wages. Prices could not be increased on any product now being produced. The business community quickly found a way to get around this directive. With a slight change in the specifications of the product being produced it was considered a new product and was not under the price controls. This demonstrated that government intervention in free market pricing is difficult to enforce. Rules were written and the enforcers were required to follow them explicitly. With the hands of the enforcers tied by the written rules, most price control rules can be disregarded by simple free market adeptness.

Most Americans believed the national economy offered unlimited opportunity. Any failure of the poor to take advantage of the economy must be due to their not assuming responsibility for themselves. Federal officials who planned the War on Poverty likewise began to share this belief. Their proposals had assumed poverty could be eliminated by teaching the poor to take advantage of the opportunities open to them. They included some financial aid to poor people in the form of the Food Stamps and Aid to Families with Dependent Children programs. They did not foresee that such aid would eventually lead to a breakdown in families. Children born to unwed mothers rose dramatically as children in their early teens realized they could receive money from the government when they had a baby. I do not believe the teenagers deliberately got pregnant, they just did nothing to prevent getting pregnant. This interrupted the education opportunities of the young teenagers which resulted in their being unable to later compete as adults in the labor market without proper education.

Job training programs were also included in the federal attempt to overcome poverty. Learning how to perform a job task was not enough, though. There had to be a job available which could be filled by the newly trained worker. When job openings which paid more than the amount a person could receive on welfare failed to appear, many of the trained workers made the decision to remain on the welfare rolls. Nothing was required of the individual to get off welfare. A large segment of the poor made the decision to become "slaves" of the United States government rather than take the low-entry jobs which would offer them the opportunity to move into higher paying jobs in the future. Individual responsibility became less of an incentive as companies with lower economic jobs would not compete with the welfare benefits which were available to the individual. It became difficult for the companies with low paying entry jobs to fill the positions necessary to operate their business. From a realistic point of view, a person with no hope of attaining much from the capitalistic system would be more willing to accept welfare money. Incentives, which are an important factor in capitalism, became less of a factor in the mind set of these individuals. They had tried once before and did not feel it was worth another attempt.

This attitude became a factor in the changing of middle class Americas's desire to help the poor. They soon became unhappy with providing financial resources for those who were not willing to help themselves. As generous as the American people are, they began to complain to congress about this growing segment of people whom they felt were abusing the intent of the system. They began to demand to congress that people on welfare should be required to do something which would enable them to get off welfare.

Television may have played a part in their thinking. During the 1930s, the public heard about the union activities through radio and newspaper reports. In the 1960s, most of the homes had television sets which showed the disturbances live in their living rooms. Many of the Americans grew disgusted with the civil rights and antiwar disturbances which they witnessed via television and formed opinions which were opposed to the activities of the radicals. Some of the social issues which were prominent at that time were affirmative action, school busing to achieve racial balance, a woman's right to have an abortion, and the desecration of the American flag by members of the radical groups. It was this last issue which angered the white working-class men. As previously stated, they began to display their anger by attacking the New Left and its allies.[3]

The majority of the Americans began to express views which were sympathetic towards the business community in America. Government intrusions into a company's right to conduct their business and the union's restrictions to work rules changes were considered detrimental to good business practices by a growing and highly educated workforce. These individuals felt their educational knowledge, which they had developed by attending college, gave them the ability to succeed without requiring a union to protect them in their employment. A growing dissatisfaction with labor activities developed in America which translated into a declining union membership during the 1980s and 1990s. The attitude that unions were unnecessary was similar to that of the 1920s workers. Prosperity seems to have a way of creating individualism in the minds of people. They feel other people are not necessary for them to gain their financial desires during prosperous times.

Chapter 10

American Capitalism Challenged by World Capitalism

Following the end of World War II, the United States became the most powerful country in the world. Policy makers of America began to formulate a policy which established a world operation of capitalism. The dollar became the dominant currency, thus becoming the basis for international exchange. The Soviet Union and later China were the only other countries with economic systems of some strength in the world which were different than capitalism.

With the increasing costs of the Vietnam War during the 1960s, a wave of inflation was set off in America which eventually began to lead to a decline in the standard of living which had been enjoyed by the American population since the end of World War II. The financial aid the United States government had extended to West Germany and Japan to guide them towards a capitalist economic system following the war began to create economic problems in America. Their modern production machinery and labor utilization without much union interference enabled West Germany and Japan to offer goods to America which were much cheaper and, in many cases better quality, than that which was produced in America's factories.

American manufacturers, with pre-war production machinery, were unable to compete with the newer machinery used in production by West Germany and Japan. They were faced with the cost of replacing their aged equipment. This presented an increase in costs of operating. Resistance by the unions to work rule changes made it difficult to attain the potential cost savings of the new equipment. Consequently, America began to lose its position as the leading producer of quality goods. With new regulations about safety in the workplace in America and new environmental rules which were being enforced, the profits began to shrink to a point where they were only one-half of what they had been earlier.[1]

It was during the 1960s and 1970s that the American manufacturers began to close their plants in the northern part of the United States and opened new plants in the south which became known as the Sun Belt. This was done to lower their labor costs which had become high in the north due to union demands. Little or no union activity was present in the Sun Belt when the manufacturers initially began the moves. A strong influx of South American and Asian immigrants had settled in the south which enabled the manufacturers to offer them jobs at wages below those of the northern workers. Those workers, at the time, had been untouched by the social demands which the northern workers stressed. This action by the manufactures allowed the workforce to increase in the south but many jobs were lost in the northern part of America. Historically, capitalists place their plants where land, labor, power, and taxes are low. On a temporary basis, America did not have a large decrease in the manufacturing jobs but, later, the capitalists would begin to shift the jobs out of the country.[2] More on this later.

Another problem in America's production was caused by the militarization of the American economy. The Cold War with the Soviet Union profoundly shaped U.S. economic priorities. With huge government contracts in hand, the American businesses focused their capital resources and technological know-how on producing armaments, especially in electronics and aviation products. This prevented the development of consumer type products. One such company which eventually disappeared as a result of the post-war commitment to military production was the Singer Sewing Machine Company. Singer sewing machines had been used throughout the world and was considered to be an example of American inventiveness in providing a product which the consumer could use productively.

Beginning in the 1970s, the many different managers of the company decided to reduce the manufacturing of their sewing machines. They began to convert the company to manufacture the less competitive and more profitable military products such as guidance systems for missiles and airplanes. With the direction towards manufacturing military products, the sales of Singer sewing machines declined dramatically. As the machinery to produce the sewing machines wore out, the managers did not replace them. This resulted in the decline of a quality product. Soon companies in Sweden and Korea began to bring their sewing machines into

America and took over the market which Singer had held for many years. When leveraged buyouts became a popular method of doing business by many companies, the name of Singer disappeared.[3]

Other economic problems appeared in America over which it had little or no control. During the war between Israel and its Arab neighbors in 1973, the Arab oil producers had formed the Organization of Petroleum Exporting Countries (OPEC). They raised the price of oil to $11.65 a barrel. This was an increase of 387 percent over the price before the war. The dramatic increase in energy costs brought about an increase in inflation throughout the world and created an inflationary recession in America. Nixon devalued the American dollar and allowed it to float in value by disconnecting it from gold. This effort to curb the rising costs and prices in America was ineffective. Wholesale prices rose 18 percent, unemployment rose to 8.5 percent, and factory output fell 10 percent in 1974.[4]

Nixon soon became engrossed with the problems of the Watergate Scandal which engulfed his administration. He lost his ability to lead the nation effectively. The problems of the economy (inflation and unemployment) were soon passed on to Vice-President Gerald Ford when President Nixon resigned on August 9, 1974.[5] Faced with the increasing inflation, Ford attempted to use persuasion as the way to curb inflation. This had no effect on the inflationary upward spiral as everyone thought individual spending should be curtailed but they felt it did not refer to them. The economy of America worsened.

New York City was an example of a city which lost control of its social structure because of the decline in their traditional industries. The decline had been the result of foreign competition of their industries' products which had forced the manufacturers to seek a cheaper labor market. Unskilled immigrants arrived to fill the low paying jobs which more skilled workers refused to perform. In the 1960s and 1970s, well meaning social programs meant that city payrolls had to be expanded to provide the staff for these programs. Also, the unions in New York City were very aggressive in their demands for higher wages which were greater than the rate of inflation.[6] As a result of the mismanagement of the city government, New York had to be "bailed out" by the federal government.

When the 1976 Presidential election was held, Ford's opponent was former Georgia governor Jimmy Carter who ran a campaign of anti-Washington and anti-incumbent rhetoric which played to the mood of the country at that time. Ford's pardon of Richard Nixon for any wrongdoing in connection with the Watergate Scandal which had run Nixon out of office, hurt him with the electorate. Carter defeated Ford in a very close electoral vote of 297 to 241 and a popular vote difference of only 2 million out of 80 million votes. The Democrats retained control of the Senate by a margin of 61 to 38 with one independent senator and continued a two to one margin in the House.[7]

When Chrysler Corporation was almost bankrupt due to Japanese imported automobiles, the company's president Lee Iacocca asked the American government for a loan which would allow him to modernize the company's plants to more effectively compete with the imported automobiles. President Carter agreed with the concept and helped Chrysler to obtain such a loan with government guarantee backing. Part of the loan agreement, though, meant that the labor union in Chrysler's plants would have to agree to lower wages.[8] They did so and Chrysler became an example of how cooperation between business, labor, and government could lead to a positive conclusion. However, it led to a strange phenomena, in my opinion. The capitalists, who constantly complain about the regulations and interference of government in America, began to request financial aid from the government whenever they wanted to build new plants or add to their present plants. In fact, some companies play the "blackmail" game by stating they will have to leave the area and move to another area where they can obtain government financial breaks. Such actions are prevalent even today.

The Carter Administration's initial attempt at slowing the rate of inflation was to ask the American businesses to reduce their spending. However, it was cheaper for companies to borrow money to conduct their business than it was to delay expenditures for new equipment and new start-up businesses which would be more expensive in the future. The public was likewise overspending due to the prospect of higher future prices for the products they wanted. They borrowed the money, either through loans or credit card purchases, which saved them money in the long run and also met the need for instantaneous gratification which had become prevalent throughout society.

In 1979, Paul Volcker was appointed to be the Chairman of the Federal Reserve Board. His quick action of using interest rates to regulate the cost of money to the business and the consumer began to have a slowing effect upon the spending for goods in America. Inflation was not curbed, though, until the interest rate was set at the 18 to 20 percent range.[9] Since the price of borrowed money is a cost in conducting business, the businessmen decided it was too costly to operate on borrowed money with such high interest rates. Many companies decided it was cheaper to forgo early payment discounts and would pay the gross amount of the invoice within the terms of the invoice. Indeed, some companies risked their good credit standing by not paying the invoice until the supplier would remind them that the invoice which had been rendered for goods and services was past due. A chain reaction by such a decision meant there were a lot of overdue invoices throughout the business community.

The consumer began to realize that making purchases on credit cards and other means of debt purchases did not give them value. They began to slow down the purchases of items "they just had to have" and confined their purchases to just the basic necessities of life. The sharp decline in spending by both the business community and the consumers brought the growing inflation to a halt. Slowly, over the next few months, the inflation rate began to ebb. Volcker had demonstrated that the best method to persuade people to slow down their spending was to make the cost of spending greater than the value received.

A very serious recession took place in America because of the interest rate tool the Federal Reserve had used. The sharp decline in business and consumer activity was considered more severe than the 1974 downturn. Thousands of business shut down. Unemployment in America soared to over 9 percent. States such as Michigan, Illinois, and Pennsylvania had double-digit unemployment figures which rivaled that of the Great Depression. This government-engineered recession continued almost unabated for the next three years. The recession had halted inflation, but at the social and economic cost of devastated cities, thousands of bankrupt firms and millions of lost job.

The fact that an unelected official of the government (Paul Volcker) was allowed to create such a situation bothered me at the time. However, I later came to realize that only an unelected official would have the courage to do so. An elected official would probably have been unable to foster the courage to deliberately bring about such a severe, but necessary, recession. It was absolutely necessary for the inflationary spiral to be stopped or America faced a bleak future. History has proven that Volcker's plan for using interest rates to control the public and business spending was instrumental in stabilizing the monetary crisis which America had faced. America was now prepared to once again take on world capitalism.

Chapter 11

A Change for the Better?

Social expectations by the American people which sprang from the civil rights and antiwar movements of the 1960s began to create a changing attitude concerning rights and entitlements among the people. We began to look upon anything which the government presented in legislation as rights instead of entitlements. Driving a car became a "right" instead of a "privilege" in the minds of some people; low cost health care was considered a "right" for living in the United States. The American people are attempting to place the ever increasing cost of health care upon the capitalists and the government. What began as a small employment benefit for the workers in years past has become a great financial burden on the profitability of many companies. Workers are resisting the requests of the companies to share a greater portion of the financial burden of health care costs. Many special interest groups in America feel business and government ought to shoulder the higher costs. Capitalism is being challenged with this unexpected problem of meeting these demands by the public.

The failure of some businessmen in the United States to be good neighbors while conducting their business activity created problems for all businessmen. Environmental issues became all encompassing legislative issues. The Occupational Safety and Health Administration was created in 1970 because a few companies failed to look upon their employees as someone who was under their care while working on their premises. This is an example of how a few CEO's failed to realize that they should conduct the business activities of their companies as though they were outsiders. They should look at the practices of their companies to determine if such practices are the way they would like to have a company treat them if they were their neighbor. After all, they live within the area and among the population.

Had the CEO's been concerned about the condition of the air surrounding their steel mills in communities such as Pittsburgh, PA,

Birmingham, AL, Middletown, OH, Newport, KY and the copper smelters in Arizona, the development of the technology to provide cleaner air would have occurred much sooner than when the government mandated it. The Clean Air and Clear Water Acts quickly followed the passage of the National Environmental Policy Act which was passed in 1970. Such an Act would have been unnecessary if the capitalists had been "better neighbors" in previous years. They must realize the government officials will respond to public demands.

The waterways in America had become polluted due to the chemical and other industrial wastes which many of America's businesses dumped into them. It was less costly for the businesses to dump their waste into the rivers than it was to properly dispose of it as they were later mandated to do. The Ohio river became so polluted with chemical waste from upriver of Cincinnati that people were advised to not eat any fish taken from the river. None of the regulations pertaining to the environment would have been put into place if the companies had been considerate of the environment. It would be much better for companies to actively improve their business environment before government forced them to do so.

Business not only pays taxes towards the cost of new government employees to implement the regulations, they also have to pay for the necessary equipment to meet the demands of the regulations. It would have been less costly for corporate America to have been considerate of the environment voluntarily. Government regulations come about because of abuses by irresponsible businesses.

This conclusion was confirmed while reading Who Built America? which I quote at this time. "Federal education, welfare, environmental and regulatory programs enacted in the late 1960s and early 1970s also translated into higher labor costs and taxes for business. Such costs—along with increasing energy prices, foreign competition, rising wages, and the failure of American business leaders to develop effective strategies to deal with those problems—seriously undermined corporate profits, which declined sharply in the 1970s. By the end of the decade, profits were approximately one-third less than they had been a generation earlier. In manufacturing, profits were only about one-half of what they had previously been.

Policy-makers in government and business agreed that the rising costs of government and declining corporate profits had to be brought under control."[1]

Ronald Reagan, an actor who had been a pro-labor liberal during the 1940s, became a militant anti-communist in the 1950s. He saw the threat of communism in Hollywood and determined he would do whatever he could to stop the spread of communism in America. Reagan became popular as a spokesman for General Electric. While Senator Barry Goldwater (R. Arizona) campaigned as the Republican presidential candidate in 1964, Reagan traveled throughout America speaking for the election of Goldwater. I met him the evening he spoke in Cincinnati at the Convention Center. Though I was apprehensive about the Goldwater candidacy, the speech Reagan presented that evening confirmed the views about personal responsibility which I have developed over the many years of my life.

The devastating defeat of Goldwater, though, did not tarnish the popularity of Reagan throughout America. He became the Republican Governor of California for two terms where he cut state spending for health, education, and welfare. In 1968, he challenged Richard Nixon for the presidential nomination. Nixon had collected political IOU's when he campaigned for many Republican office holders in previous years. The calling in of the IOU's by Nixon at the 1968 convention prevented Reagan from receiving the nomination that year.

Failure to receive the presidential nomination in 1968 did not stop Reagan's quest for the office of President of the United States. Though the Republican Party had been tarnished by the Watergate Scandal of 1972, Reagan's ability to communicate to people enabled him to obtain the Republican nomination for President in 1980. During the election campaign between Reagan and President Carter, labor and the general public had turned to the right of the political spectrum. The change in the public's political views led to a decline in Carter's popularity in the polls. He had also encountered the seizure of the U.S. Embassy in Iran. The American personnel at the embassy were held hostage until the end of his term. Ronald Reagan was elected in November 1980. In a show of contempt towards

Carter, the Iranians released the hostages on the day Reagan was inaugurated.

Early in President Reagan's presidency, he was able to obtain a dramatic change in the tax rates and incentives for all citizens, including the business establishments, in America. He believed in the "trickle down" theory which Herbert Hoover had used during the initial stages of the Great Depression in the 1930s. Initially there was little reaction towards the tax incentives in the business community. America was still in the throes of the severe recession which had begun under Carter. Figuratively speaking, the American businessmen stuck the money in their pockets and walked away awaiting better economic times to use the incentives. First impression was that once again the "trickle down" theory had failed. However, when the effects of the recession began to ebb, the theory began to take hold. New types of business operations began to appear.

One of the new tax incentives permitted businesses to depreciate new equipment costs over a shorter time period. Enterprising businessmen studied the marketplace. They found that companies purchased some equipment but did not use it on a constant basis. With the new depreciation tax rules and other incentives, the enterprising businessmen found they could purchase such equipment, lease it to several companies on an "as needed basis" while depreciating it over the new shorter time period. The companies which were willing to lease equipment as the need arose realized it was no longer necessary to tie up company funds by purchasing such equipment. Even though they could have depreciated the equipment over a shorter period of time, the cost of the lease was a current expense for doing business. Using leased equipment to replace purchased equipment required only sparingly increased their profits. Some of the companies who were already in the business of renting small tools for the "handyman" to use around the home expanded into heavy equipment. When a person drives by these companies, it is not unusual to see large pieces of equipment which construction companies had to own in the past. Now the construction companies lease the equipment when the need arises.

During the early 1980s, companies aggressively began to change their work environment. Concessions in work rules and wages had been granted to the companies by the unions because of the severe recession. Reagan demonstrated a new toughness toward labor when the Professional Air Traffic Controllers' Organization (PATCO) went on strike in August 1981 to protest the mental strain under which they were forced to work. He told them to return to work within ten days or he would hire replacement workers to take their place. When they did not return to work, replacement air traffic controllers were hired, trained and put to work. The striking air controllers were informed of their termination.

Leaders of other companies followed the example of breaking the PATCO union. An early casualty among unions was the Greyhound Bus Line. When the workers were asked to take wage reductions by management, they rejected the request and went on strike. After a period of time, management sent each striking driver a letter informing them they must return to work within ten days or replacement drivers would be hired to take their place. Union leaders had gone through such threats in the past and refused to allow the union drivers to return to work. They wanted to continue negotiating but management began hiring new drivers after ten days. A shockwave went throughout the unions when new drivers were willing to cross the picket lines. The unions leaders failed to realize there was a large surplus of unemployed workers left over from the severe recession who were looking for jobs. Honoring a union picket line was no longer a consideration for an unemployed worker who would do anything for a job.

Thus began a new era of labor/management relations. Management more or less told the workers, "If you don't like working here, leave. I can always get someone else to take your place." With union membership being only 16 percent of the 101 million workers, they had begun to lose their clout. Management was now back in the "cat bird's seat" so to speak. The new managers of American companies now looked upon the human element in production as something to eliminate in their quest to reduce costs.

As a Production Control Manager/Purchasing Manager during this period, I was able to observe the change taking place in the work environment in America. During my thirty-seven year career, I noticed that business is conducted like a game. Whatever theory was popular at the present time, it was adopted by most of the other companies. In the early years of my career, I noticed most CEO's in the 1950s came from a sales background. Later, when the demand for increasing productivity and quality became the game, the Board of Directors selected persons with an engineering background to be the CEO's. The decisions made by the CEO's with sales and engineering credentials were profit oriented but were also directed towards establishing long term relations with their customers.

During the 1980s, a change in the attitude of the companies towards their customers took place. It appeared to match the same relationship the companies had with their workers. When I asked the salesmen who had ordered the changes in sales policies that were taking place, almost all of them said it was the new Chief Financial Officer or new Chief Executive Officer who had risen from the accounting ranks. With the shrinking profits which had taken place in industry during the previous decade, accountants were being called upon by upper management to determine how best to increase the profit margins. Young accounting managers with MBA's began to move up the corporate ladder quickly until they became the CEO's or were placed in the position of CFO's by the company's Board of Directors. As the CFO's, they were given much authority in the manufacturing and sales of the products their company was producing. Since the accountants had little training in establishing relationships with customers, the customers soon discovered they were made to feel unimportant. This was my experience and many other purchasing managers I spoke to at that time said they were also experiencing the new attitude the suppliers were showing toward them.

After this change was made, the companies in America became what I refer to as "lean and mean". The bottom line appeared to become an altar at which the new managers of companies worshiped. Wherever possible, the human element was eliminated. The productivity (an accounting term) within the country increased dramatically which enabled the companies to compete with the invasion of foreign products. The managers also looked to Mexico and other countries for the possibility of building factories in their country. American capitalists were on the move out of America.

They remembered how productive it had been to shut down plants in the northern part of the United States and build new plants in the southern and southwestern states. Receiving financial and tax assistance from states asking them to move their operating facilities within their borders to provide jobs for their citizens had been the game at that time. Now the capitalists were ready to expand the game and make such moves to other countries.

It was during this time that I became disappointed in the demeanor of the American capitalists. In a controlled capitalism environment, I believe that society as a whole prospers. The prosperity involves both companies and individual people. It was when the "me first" attitude, which had been given birth in the 1970s, reached the higher levels of corporate life that cooperation within the business world began to deteriorate. With "teamwork" giving way to a "dog eat dog attitude", a decline in business ethics began to appear. For many years, I had never found it necessary to sign a contract with a supplier because of the integrity found in the business world. It now became necessary for me to sign contracts to protect the company for which I worked. I wondered if America was slipping back to the late 1800s.

A growing distrust of people in influential positions began to take place. My retirement at age 60 in January 1992 was brought about by my disapproval of the change I was beginning to see take place in America's political and business environment. It did not surprise me when William Jefferson Clinton was elected President in November 1992. The people of America were willing to take a chance on an unknown person instead of sticking with George H. W. Bush who had been a very popular president due to the success of the Gulf War.

When Clinton was elected to the office of President, he surrounded himself with people who believed in more and greater government involvement in the lives of the American people. Government regulations, which had been passed during the time of "social consciousness" in the 1970s, began to interfere with the lives of the common person in America. This came about as the bureaucrats who fostered greater government involvement in the lives of people began to interpret the regulations with their personal biases. When the government began to tell people how they could or could not use their private property, the general public began to complain to their congressional representatives in Washington. Nothing came out of the complaints during Clinton's first two years except a furthering distrust of politicians and bureaucrats in Washington.

With the political spectrum already moving towards a more conservative tone, Newt Gingrich, a Republican conservative congressman from Georgia, lead a national crusade during the 1994 congressional campaign which the Republicans called "A Contract With America". Despite the fact that Clinton spoke from the center of the political spectrum, his administration governed from the left of center. The American voters chose to elect a more conservative congress hoping to rescind many of the intrusive regulations which were being interpreted with a more liberal bias by the administration. Some of the regulations which had angered the people in the street were changed by congress to be less intrusive. During this time of changing or removing regulations, the business community entered the process of redefining regulations. Some of the regulations which restricted businesses in conducting their business activities were modified or removed by congress. Capitalism in America was becoming less regulated.

As the pace of deregulation took place in the 1990s, it appeared the latest method of doing business would be successful. The economy began to soar with the stock market rising to levels never before seen in America. The people were unaware that a scandal was developing beneath the surface of some of the companies which had been started in the deregulated energy and telecommunication industries. The scandal is playing out at this time. Companies such as Enron, World Com, Global Crossing, adelphia and others have disclosed they misused proper accounting procedures in their financial reports. Much of the accounting advise in using these improper accounting procedures appears to have come from a large national accounting firm. Perhaps this is the penalty we must pay for America's companies placing too much trust and authority in the hands of accountants who appear to manage with very narrow views.

The government is presently investigating the improprieties and also determining if there were any government officials involved. Should any criminal activities be discovered, all those who were involved should be placed on trial. If found guilty, they should be sentenced to prison terms which are long enough to discourage future political and business people from looking for schemes to get rich by bending and/or manipulating the rules and laws of America. Such action by the government was taken in the late 1800s and early 1900s after the public outcry against the wrongs in the business world had surfaced. Political leaders of both parties stepped forward at that time with a show of non-partisan statesmanship. Let us hope this same kind of statesmanship comes forward this time.

I mention this only because it has been stated that the national accounting firm was not only the auditor of the companies books but was also receiving compensation to be their accounting advisers. Congress has passed a reform bill which prohibits such practice in the future. Even though many people look upon regulations as a constraint in conducting business, these latest incidents have proven there must be some degree of control over capitalism to protect the public from unscrupulous activity by leaders of commerce.

As the research for this book developed, I noticed an interesting change in describing the economic cycles which had occurred in America. Prior to 1932, which I allege was the beginning of controlling capitalism, all the down business cycles were called Panics or Depressions because of their severity. Since 1932, all the down cycles have been called Recessions. A recession is just a pause in an economic cycle created by an imbalance of inventories. During the pause, companies and retailers adjust their inventories to meet the current market demand. Panics and depressions are caused by forces outside of the normal conduct of the market. Those forces have to be corrected before there is an opportunity for the return of growth in the marketplace.

Have forces outside of the normal conduct of the marketplace entered into the present day economic cycle? Looking at the 1920s historically, I see a great deal of similarities between those years and the 1990s. During both of the decades, everyone believed there was only one direction for the economy to go and that was up, up, and up further. Young investors of today entered the stock market through their 401k's and IRA's. Their portfolios increased dramatically as stock prices climbed for the new unregulated companies and the technology companies which had been founded by many of the new breed of young entrepreneurs. The prices soared beyond reasonable levels. Many companies which had not earned a profit for years continued to be priced in the $100 a share range. The earnings/price ratio, which investors use to determine the value of a company's stock, was at astronomical levels for some of these companies.

Profit sharing plans and pension plans also generated new money to be placed in the stock market. A percentage of this new money was entered into the stock-market through the Mutual Funds industry. This created problems for the managers of said funds. As the new money arrived, the managers of the funds were forced to invest it for the benefit of the investors. Rules of certain funds forced the managers to invest the new money into stocks even though it was apparent the prices of stocks were too high. It became more difficult to find stocks of companies which would provide a decent return to the investor. Demand for stocks was greater than the supply, consequently, the stock-market continued to rise.

When September 11, 2001 occurred, everything came to a stand still on Wall Street. As the possibility of further terrorists problems in America developed, nervous managers and investors began to sell stocks they controlled or owned. That created a tremendous sell off which in turn fed a further sell off. The stock-market suffered dramatically and people wondered when it would stop. Many young investors were learning that the stock market does not always go upward. They found that events outside of the investment world could cause the stock-market to decline. When such events create an emotional environment, the decline in the stock market is usually more rapid and deeper than that found in a rising stock market. If there is one good thing which has come out of the current state of the stock-market, it is the experience the younger generation has received in the techniques and methods of investing.

One factor in the stock-market which is different when comparing the 1920s and 1990s investors in stocks is the margin method of buying stocks. Money placed in 401K's, company Profit Sharing Plans, company Pension Plans and individual IRA's is 100% money. During the 1920s, a great deal of the money invested in the stock-market was on a 10% margin. The value of the stock-market depended upon the ability of the investor to come up with more money to cover the margin should the stock prices decline. That was not true with the 1990s stock-market. With huge sums of money invested through the above mentioned methods, there was no fear of forced sales. The only forced sales came when individual investors made the decision to move their investments from mutual funds to cash funds. Some mutual funds were forced to make sales to raise the cash to permit such transitions. My observation at the time of the tremendous decline was of the amount of good money which was available to stop the decline even though it was at a much lower level.

Chapter 12

Capitalism and Politics in America Today

Having read many books and articles over several years trying to determine why we have such a high standard of living in America, I have reached the conclusion that one of the significant reasons is our controlling of the capitalistic economic system in our country. The slogan "controlled capitalism" seems to best describe capitalism in America. To me, that meant the capitalists would be free to operate in the United States but their business activities would be controlled in a manner which would benefit both them and society as a whole. By controlling capitalism through the use of the Executive, Legislative and Judicial branches of our government, the people have allowed capitalism to flourish as an entity but does not permit their exploitation of the people.

It is my good fortune to have lived during the time in America's history when this tremendous increase took place. Much of the groundwork to attain this quality of life we have today in America was laid by previous generations. Those generations paid a heavy price while battling the capitalists for a greater share of the wealth which was being created. Some lives were lost and much financial losses were incurred during lengthy strikes which occurred while attempting to resolve the differences between capitalists and labor. All Americans, including new immigrants, should recognize this fact.

Our country began with a strong sense of "individualism". The pioneers of what was to become known as the United States of America established this nation on July 4, 1776 when they rendered a Declaration of Independence from England. After a long war to affirm this Declaration of Independence, the leaders of the new nation wrote a Constitution of the United States which was approved on September 17, 1787. They had a vision where the people would decide the destiny of the new country which had been formed following that Revolutionary War.

The Constitution was one of the most perfect, yet incomplete, documents which has ever been written. Knowing that social structures change, they put within the document a means by which the people could make changes which would improve upon the Constitution they had written. They provided a lengthy process by which the changes could be made, thus preventing whimsical changes which were the result of an emotional event. Only those changes which a large majority of Americans agreed upon could become part of the Constitution.

By March 4, 1789, the Congress of the United States had developed and approved a "Bill of Rights" which became part of the Constitution of the United States. Those Rights were adopted to prevent the abuse of power by the newly found government. The first two Articles of the Bill of Rights were not ratified by Congress. Following the two Articles which were rejected are the ten Articles by which we Americans have lived since their conception. These two documents have protected all individuals successfully from any government action without the due process of law. The concept and words of these trustworthy documents have made this country the world's most sought after place to live.

Freedom to live the life we each choose sometimes creates problems within our society but we do not stifle the rights of each person to live as they choose. However, certain events in our history created an environment where the people were forced to use the due process of law to make our country a better place to live. Such an event was when some capitalists felt it was their right of individuality to take advantage of American workers.

The one major negative characteristic of capitalism, in my opinion, is the opportunity for exploiting large segments of society by a small number of individuals due to their greed for power and money. Money by itself is not inherently evil. It is the love of it without any concern for the welfare of others which causes social problems in the world. America has always admired the ability of individuals to be creative. Without such individuals, our country would not have advanced so rapidly to such a high standard of living. However, in the early stages of our country's history, certain individuals used their talents to gain considerable wealth by unscrupulous means. In the process of gaining their wealth, they used the work skills of people without consideration of the workers' contribution towards creating a value in the product or service.

With the continuing arrivals of immigrants during the early stages of the industrialization of America, capitalists used the different ethnic backgrounds of the immigrants as a means to hold down wages in the production of goods and services. Using government officials, the capitalists selected certain countries from which they wanted to receive immigrants, i.e. Chinese to build the railroads. By taking advantage of the different ethnic groups, the disparity between the "haves and have nots" continued to widen.

As the immigrants began to understand the Constitution of the United States, the determination to use its protection to better the lives of the workers grew. The workers of America started to challenge the complete control the capitalists had over their lives. Early attempts to prevent labor from organizing were met with both verbal and physical conflicts between owners and laborers. Owners felt everything which had to do with their company was protected by the constitutional rights of property. The "establishment" used their positions of power to elect government legislative bodies which enacted laws prohibiting or deterring the workers efforts to gain "their fair share" of the wealth being created in America.

This would be changed when the American workers began to use the ballot box to their advantage. Nothing changed overnight but the slow process of the people of America gaining control of the capitalistic system began to move forward. As each new generation became more educated, they gained the knowledge of how to best use the Constitution to protect their rights as presented in the Bill of Rights. However, the vast majority of the growing population were never inclined to replace capitalism with another economic system.

During the evolution from the beginning of capitalism in America to the present role of capitalism today, there were many bumps in the road. A few of the bumps were caused by the activities of individuals such as the "Robber Barons". Though each of them possessed the necessary personality characteristics to become successful businessmen, they appeared to lack the one personality trait which would have made them great in the eyes of *all* Americans. That trait was the lack of understanding that success may be obtained without using corrupt methods. The bribing of government officials and using unscrupulous methods of dealing with competitors, which some or all of them used during their rise to great wealth, was unnecessary. However, as they began to come to the end of their lives, some of them appeared to use philanthropy to ease their conscience.

In mentioning the bribing and unscrupulous methods used in business and politics which occurred in those days, I would like to point out that it always required two people to do so. One was the individual seeking to gain an advantage in business practices and the other was the individual using their political position to gain monetary wealth. This unethical use of their positions is not limited to just capitalism. Any economic system has unsavory individuals who feel it is their right to make money in any manner they choose without regard as to whether it is done in an ethical or unethical manner.

I would like to present my views of capitalism, socialism, and communism as economic systems. Those individuals who are in control of the money supply and the distribution of it are basically the capitalists within any economic system. In capitalism, individuals are the distributors of the capital they have attained through personal accumulation from means of production or use of private property. Government is not involved in the means of production or private property but are responsible for providing a sound currency which can be used by the individual capitalists.

Socialism is an economic system where the means of major production or service are owned by the government but there is some ownership of private property permitted. The distribution of capital is through bureaucrats who work for the government which controls the money supply. Bureaucrats are required to follow written rules and laws to the letter, thus preventing independent reaction to events which occur in the market place.

Communism, likewise, is the distributor of capital through government bureaucrats but there is no private ownership of property. Decisions for the use of the capital is made by bureaucrats who must follow the dictates of the political leaders who have their own agenda. To assure the continuity of such an economic system, individual freedoms are not permitted.

It is my contention, therefore, that a society must determine how they wish to distribute the capital within their economic system. My personal preference is to let non-governmental individuals be the distributors of capital. The market-place determines how it is best distributed and is more attuned to the desires and needs of a society. Perhaps it is this personal bias towards capitalism which has produced my affirmative conclusion that "controlled capitalism" is the best economic system under which a society can live.

I challenge anyone to show me an economic system which produces as much overall wealth for the people as does that which is exemplary in America. Where else has a people such as the African-Americans had the *opportunity* to rise from complete slavery to *ownership* of job creating companies in less than 150 years. I am proud to live in a country where such freedom and wealth opportunities permitted this to occur following the Civil War though it has been a long and hard struggle which continues even to this day.

The reason I prefer private individuals distributing the capital is simple. To obtain the capital necessary for any business enterprise I desire to become involved in is based upon whether the capitalists believe they can profit from my ability to be successful. If they believe in my ability, they will loan me the capital at an interest rate commensurate with the risk. That is the bottom line. In socialism, I would have to deal with a government worker who must follow written rules and regulations to the letter to determine if I should be allowed to obtain any capital. There can be no deviation from the rules and regulations by a government worker even if the individual personally believed my idea would be successful. In communism, everything is owned by the state, therefore, I would have no opportunity to go out on my own.

In the pursuit to control capitalism in America, it became necessary for the workers to use the ballot box and the government to bring about a change in the way capitalism functioned. Sometimes these efforts were met with violence as the workers attempted to receive a more equitable share of the wealth they were creating for the capitalists. It is fortunate for America that the love for the freedoms which are guaranteed by our Constitution was considered by all involved whenever violence did break out.

The unions originally gave the workers the strength to overcome the appalling conditions under which they had to work. Some unions leaders eventually used this strength for their personal gains. Yes, the workers benefitted by the monetary gains and work rule changes their leaders attained for them through negotiations with the management of companies. They looked the other way, however, when the "free" news media pointed out some of the corrupt means by which the labor leaders were gaining personal wealth. This began to change the public's perception about the value of the union movement. The pendulum of history began to swing away from collective workers strength to individualism within the workforce. The result was a decline in union membership.

Through the years, capitalism was challenged throughout the world. Communism failed in the Soviet Union and other countries so the communist economic system was not the answer to many of the social problems in the world. Capitalism has been accused of creating the poverty levels throughout the Third World countries. It is my contention that "uncontrolled capitalism", where only the fittest survive, **may** be part of the problem.

If the leaders of the world had studied what made America the strong economic power it is, they would have discovered a very simple formula. The government should provide education opportunity for all the people. An educated society makes for a strong society. The capitalists would then have a workforce which could contribute in this industrial and technological world we live in today. By providing an educated workforce, it is imperative that the governments allow the capitalists to operate their companies but there must be a means to control the greed factor which exists in all people. Some rules and regulations should be in place to protect society but not to the extent that growth within the capitalistic system would be stifled.

When the capitalists in America began moving some of their manufacturing operations to lesser developed countries, the wages they paid their workers were comparable to what the workers were paid in the early years of America's industrial growth. Their workers were unable to purchase the very products they were producing due to the low wages they were receiving. If the industrialists would pay wages which enabled the workers the opportunity to purchase the goods they produced, a market would be created within that country. The earnings of the companies which the industrialists operated would have increased as their market expanded. Henry Ford invested in labor and benefitted greatly because of it.

Many of the manufacturing jobs in America have been eliminated because of the American capitalists taking those jobs overseas. Manufacturing of critical products needed in America has been placed in the hands of countries which are not necessarily favorable to us. A large percentage of the basic materials used in America, such as steel, is being imported from other countries. Soon we will be in a situation similar to that of the oil market. Our economic security will be in the hands of other countries.

Much of the job growth in America is in the service area. Unfortunately there are many people in America who are not prepared to perform those service jobs. Not all people are inclined towards technology jobs. An increasing number of Americans are becoming unhappy because they are unable to find jobs for which they are qualified. The retraining of those people will be expensive. Is this the time for capitalism to step forward to help provide the financial resources needed to retrain the workers to meet the skills required for the new jobs? Should they choose to not be involved in the massive retraining of the workers, the government will do so but possibly not in the manner which would be beneficial towards capitalism.

It is important for the American people to pay close attention to what will be said during the upcoming election in 2004. The Democrat Party appears to be leaning towards changing our capitalistic system to a socialist form of government and economic system in America. Some liberal Democrat members of congress advocate the federal government providing us with all our needs as **they** see them. Some of the conservative Republican members of congress appear to advocate dismantling much of the progress our country has made while controlling capitalism. Other conservative voices can be heard advocating a government which would allow the capitalists to operate without any controls. They believe in using the free market to determine our destiny. A free market, without any attempt to control it, will lead to the booms and busts of the past. I, for one, do not agree with a totally free market.

Voters of both parties have to be aware of where their party leaders are taking this great nation called America. Socialism (or ultra-liberalism) will use the government to provide jobs but deny us the many freedoms we presently enjoy. Capitalism (or ultra-conservatism) will deny us the many job related gains which have been accomplished over the past decades. We should never allow either party to take our country to the extreme economic positions which is presently advocated by ultra-conservatives and ultra-liberals. Senator Barry Goldwater was vilified for saying that extremism in the quest for freedom is not wrong. That statement is correct when taken in proper context but extremism by either party while performing the normal act of governing a people who already have freedom *is* wrong. Extremism in either political view could lead to a loss of our freedoms such as we know them to be.

In my opinion, as an educated person who has experienced life in America for over seventy years, the extremes of the ultra-liberals and ultra-conservatives are not healthy. The debates between the two extremes are helpful, though, as a means for the vast majority of Americans to obtain, sort out, and use the good viewpoints of the two philosophies. Then we, as responsible citizens of America, will be capable of providing a great future for the people who are yet to be born. Will the election of 2004 be an election to decide which form of government and economic system America will have in the future? Is the time that close?

As you may have surmised while reading this book, I am a strong advocate of the unions in America. There were times I became upset when union leaders abused their position for personal financial gain. I felt they should be punished by the justice system for those abuses. However, it is my personal view that without the unions being a part of the effort to control capitalism in America, we ordinary citizens would not have the standard of living we presently enjoy.

Unfortunately the unions began to abuse the power they had attained over the years. Like anyone who gains too much power they began to reach too far in their demands. The general public began to feel the workers had become too extreme. When that occurred, the power of the unions began to decline. In an election campaign, a candidate who speaks out strongly for unionism does not necessarily approve of the excessive power the unions exercise nor should they be considered socialists. By observing the candidates' political record, it should be possible to determine if their rhetoric is extreme in either direction.

The center of America's political spectrum is where the people have voted to reject the extreme views of both the ultra-liberals (socialists) and the ultra-conservatives (uncontrolled capitalism). This can be confirmed by looking back at recent history. Senator Barry Goldwater was rejected in 1964 because of his extreme conservative views. President Lyndon Johnson used an extremely liberal congress during 1965-66 to pass much liberal legislation, including the "War on Poverty". During the next congressional election in November 1966, the American people spoke by electing many less liberal congressmen. These congressmen joined others in curtailing some of the extreme liberal legislative programs President Johnson had succeeded in getting passed by the previous congress.

I realize my views are of a dream world but we can begin to reach towards it by retaining America's style of capitalism. We must show the world that our economic system and form of government would be successful throughout the world without trampling on other's cultures. The people of the world, both leaders and ordinary citizens, should study America's past history to determine how we succeeded in controlling capitalism.

Our success provided us with the greatest standard of living in the history of mankind. Where we have had weaknesses, others can overlook or strengthen them; where we have had turmoil, they can work on relationships to prevent turmoil from occurring within their country. It must be remembered, though, that they are dealing with people. As we all know, America is constantly examining its weaknesses and strengths to determine what its future will hold.

We who live in the United States of America are being watched by the rest of the world. It is our responsibility to show them that the political freedom of our Constitution and capitalism, which is permitted to flourish but not allowed to exploit the people, as our economic system, really does work when the people desire it and demand it of their political and business leaders.

Source Notes

Chapter 1

[1] A People's History of the United States 1492-Present (Revised and updated edition), pg. 214 - Howard Zinn - First HarperPerennial edition published 1995
[2] Howard Zinn 214
[3] A History of the American People, pgs. 537-568 - Paul Johnson - First HarperPerennial edition published 1999
[4] Paul Johnson 537
[5] Paul Johnson 538
[6] Paul Johnson 539
[7] Paul Johnson 540
[8] Howard Zinn 248
[9] Paul Johnson 540
[10] Paul Johnson 542
[11] Paul Johnson 543
[12] Paul Johnson 543
[13] Paul Johnson 551
[14] Paul Johnson 552
[15] Howard Zinn 251
[16] Howard Zinn 251
[17] Paul Johnson 551-552
[18] PBS Online/WGBH - Documentary "Meet Andrew Carnegie - The Two Andrews"
[19] Howard Zinn
[20] Paul Johnson 556-557
[21] Paul Johnson 557
[22] Paul Johnson 564
[23] Paul Johnson 564-565
[24] The Almanac of American History, pg. 327 - Arthur M. Schlesinger, Jr.- Editor - copyright 1993 by Brompton Books Corporation - Publisher Barnes & Noble, Inc.
[25] Paul Johnson 602603

[26] Don't Know Much About History, pg. 203 - Kenneth C. Davis - copyright 1990 by Kenneth C. Davis - Published by Avon Books printing June 1991
[27] Paul Johnson 603
[28] Howard Zinn 248
[29] Howard Zinn 248
[30] Arthur M. Schlesinger, Jr. 341
[31] Paul Johnson 580
[32] Paul Johnson 580-581
[33] Paul Johnson 581
[34] Paul Johnson 581
[35] http://encarta.msn.com/encnet/features/Reference.aspk (Search - Thomas A. Edison)
[36] http://encarta.msn.com/encnet/features/Reference.aspk (Search - Henry Ford)
[37] Paul Johnson 606
[38] Paul Johnson 606-607
[39] Paul Johnson 607
[40] American History, August 2003, page 18

Chapter 2

[1] Who Built America? Volume Two, pg. 99 - American Social History Productions, Inc., The City University of New York - Herbert G. Gutman, Founding Director - Stephen Brier, Project Director and Supervising Editor - contributing writers Joshua Freeman, Nelson Lichtenstein, Stephen Brier, David Bensman, Susan Porter Benson, David Brundage, Bret Eynon, Bruce Levine, Bryan Palmer, with Joshua Brown who was Visual Editor and Roy Rosenzweig as the Consulting Editor - Pantheon Books, New York 1992
[2] Who Built America? 99
[3] Who Built America? 69
[4] Who Built America? 69
[5] Who Built America? 70
[6] Who Built America? 72

[7] Who Built America? 73
[8] Who Built America? 111
[9] Who Built America? 111
[10] Who Built America? 117
[11] Who Built America? 111-112
[12] Who Built America? 73-74
[13] Who Built America? 74-75
[14] Gompers
http://www.stfrancis.edu/ba/ghkickul/stuwebs/bbios/biograph/samuel
l.html
[15] Gompers http:// ...samuel
[16] Arthur Schlesinger, Jr. 348
[17] Kenneth Davis 209

Chapter 3

[1] Paul Johnson 600
[2] Paul Johnson 600
[3] Who Built America? 123
[4] Who Built America? 126
[5] Who Built America? 126
[6] Who Built America? 126
[7] Who Built America? 127-128
[8] Who Built America? 133
[9] Who Built America? 133-134
[10] Who Built America? 134

Chapter 4

[1] Kenneth Davis 211
[2] Kenneth Davis 211
[3] Who Built America? 138
[4] Who Built America? 139
[5] Paul Johnson 601

[6] Arthur Schlesinger, Jr. 408
[7] Who Built America? 130-131
[8] Who Built America? 209
[9] Who Built America? 209-210
[10] Who Built America? 210
[11] Arthur Schlesinger, Jr. 417
[12] Arthur Schlesinger, Jr. 422
[13] Arthur Schlesinger, Jr. 423
[14] Who Built America? 212
[15] Who Built America? 213
[16] Who Built America? 213

Chapter 5

[1] Arthur M. Schlesinger, Jr. 440-441
[2] Paul Johnson 715
[3] Paul Johnson 717
[4] Arthur M. Schlesinger, Jr. 444
[5] Arthur M. Schlesinger, Jr. 452
[6] Arthur M. Schlesinger, Jr. 454
[7] ?

Chapter 6

[1] Arthur M. Schlesinger, Jr. 438
[2] Who Built America? 334-335
[3] MSN Learning & Research - Stalin, Joseph –
http://encarta.msn.com/refpages 3 & 4
[4] Who Built America? 346
[5] Who Built America? 347
[6] Who Built America? 351-353
[7] Who Built America? 353
[8] Who Built America? 356
[9] Who Built America> 356-357

[7] Truman - pg. 898 - David McCullough - copyright 1992 - Published by Simon & Schuster
[8] Arthur M. Schlesinger, Jr. 531
[9] Arthur Schlesinger, Jr. 555-556

Chapter 9

[1] Arthur Schlesinger, Jr. 587
[2] Who Built America? 604
[3] Who Built America? 604

Chapter 10

[1] Who Built America? 615
[2] Who Built America? 616
[3] Who Built America? 611-612
[4] Paul Johnson 902-903
[5] Arthur Schlesinger, Jr. 599
[6] Who Built America? 618
[7] Arthur Schlesinger, Jr. 603
[8] Arthur Schlesinger, Jr. 605-606
[9] Who Built America? 620

Chapter 11

[1] Who Built America? 614-615

About the Author

Warren E. Peterson worked 37 years as a Production Control Manager and Purchasing Manager. He was active in the Cincinnati Purchasing Managers Association where he led Workshops and wrote articles concerning good purchasing practices for their magazine. After retiring in 1992, he read several books about the history of America to learn more about capitalism in the country. He has used his business experiences and knowledge gained from his readings to compile a history of the struggle by the American people to gain a fair share of the wealth created by their work. Today he is concerned that capitalism is becoming less controlled. He wonders if America would turn to socialism if capitalism attempts to roll back time too far.